# The Covenant with the Jews

D1324235

# The Covenant with the Jews

## What's So Unique About The Jewish People?

**WALTER RIGGANS**

MONARCH PUBLICATIONS
Tunbridge Wells

First published 1992

*Front cover photos*
*Western wall: Cephas Picture Library*
*World map: Tony Stone Photolibrary, London*

ISBN 1 85424 188 5

Unless otherwise indicated, biblical quotations are from the
New International Version © 1973, 1978, 1984 by the
International Bible Society.

**British Library Cataloguing in Publication Data**
A catalogue record for this book is available from
the British Library.

Production and Printing in England for
MONARCH PUBLICATIONS
Owl Lodge, Langton Road, Speldhurst, Kent TN3 0NP
by Nuprint Ltd, Harpenden, Herts AL5 4SE

# THE ALL NATIONS SERIES

All Nations Booklets aim to:

1. Provide basic teaching on various aspects of mission
2. Raise awareness of the importance of mission in Western churches
3. Stimulate support for mission through prayer and action
4. Help churches in the multi-cultural West to learn from the experiences of churches worldwide.

# CONTENTS

# INTRODUCTION

*Jewish* people will give different answers to the question which forms the sub title of this book. Depending on whom you ask, you will be supplied with answers as varied as the following, all of which have often been said to the present writer:

> 'We are the chosen people of God.'
> 'We have kept the covenant of God down through the generations.'
> 'We are a mini-civilisation, with something to contribute to other civilisations.'
> 'We are the scapegoats for other peoples' problems.'
> 'We are just the descendants of Abraham, Isaac, and Jacob.'

Not all Jewish people are concerned to practise the faith of Judaism, and certainly not according to the definition of Orthodox Judaism. For some, the importance of being Jewish is bound up solely with the cultural aspects of their community life. In the

West, however, increasing numbers of Jewish people are showing that they are not too concerned at all about being Jewish, since they are happy to marry non-Jewish partners and live lives which seem to all intents and purposes to be indistinguishable from those of non-Jews.

If a survey were to be done with a cross-section of *non-Jewish* people, there would also be a spread of answers given to the question concerning what is so special about the Jewish people. Here is another list of responses from my own experience and conversations:

> 'The only special thing is that they think they're special.'
> 'There's nothing special about them.'
> 'They control the banks and the media.'
> 'They're sort of exclusive and clannish.'
> 'They're the cause of the problems in the Middle East.'
> 'They really care about each other.'

Some of these responses reflect the tragically common attitude of antisemitism, while others reveal that people have swallowed the propaganda fed to them by antisemites. Of course some people just don't know anything about the distinctives of the Jewish people and their traditions.

*Christians* also share a variety of responses to the question. It is far from uncommon to hear the following things said, even from the pulpit:

> 'They are the chosen people of God.'
> 'They rejected God and killed Jesus.'

'They keep trying to earn their way to heaven.'

'One day they will have to acknowledge who Jesus is.'

'There's nothing special about them—any more.'

As far as Christians are concerned, these responses, and the many others which are made, come partly from certain theological understandings of the Bible and Christian self-identity, partly from insecurity about those understandings, partly from out-and-out ignorance, and partly from the dreadful sin of antisemitism, which has been, and continues to be, endemic within the Church. In this book we shall be looking particularly at the issue of the relationship between Israel and the *Church*, and so our immediate concern is the *Christian* attitude to the Jewish people. The perspective of the series of books to which this one belongs is that of evangelical Christianity, so it is hoped that that sector of the Church will find it especially helpful.

In such an introductory book we will have to be content with general descriptions, principles and contexts, but we will, nevertheless, manage to examine the basic issues which affect the ways that Jews and Christians view one another. It may well be, for instance, that some Christians will be asking themselves why we need a book at all about the Jewish people. Isn't it just as important to have something on the very distinct Buddhist traditions, or those of the various tribes of Africa? It certainly is important, and indeed each culture, each religion, each worldview, must be studied carefully and properly if Christians are to relate with love and respect to the peoples involved. However, if one can coin a phrase, there is something 'uniquely unique' about the Jewish people and their religious traditions, something which makes it absolutely essential that Christians come to terms with the relationship between the Church and Israel.

In his letter to the Romans Paul wrote of the people of Israel in the following terms:

> Theirs is the adoption as sons; theirs the divine glory, the covenants, the receiving of the law, the temple worship and the promises. Theirs are the patriarchs, and from them is traced the human ancestry of Christ, who is God over all, for ever praised! Amen (Rom 9:4–5).

Notice that Paul is using the present tense throughout this statement. He does not teach us that Israel *used* to be special in the world, but that she still maintains that uniqueness, in some sense at least. Only the Jewish people can claim to have *priority* in their disagreements with Christians over matters of theology. Only Israel can say that she was there first! When Christians speak about the Bible as the word of God, about the central truths of God as our Creator and Redeemer, or about God's purposes in history, about how God intervenes in people's lives, about the basic principles of the true worship and service of God, or about the nature and work of the Messiah, etc, then only the Jewish people can say to them that they were in a living relationship with this God, and in possession of this knowledge even before the Church came into being.

Christians, therefore, must take the Jewish challenge to the Gospel very seriously indeed. Our very identity as the people of God is bound up with the identity of Israel and the continued vitality of Judaism. It becomes obvious then why Paul insists that the Gospel is the power of God for the salvation of everyone, but 'first for the Jew, then for the Gentile' (Rom 1:16). To put it in other words, if the great majority of Jesus' own people have refused to accept him as God's Messiah, why should anyone else accept him? If Jesus has nothing to say to Jewish people, then he has nothing to say to anyone!

As we move into the body of this book, the following issues will be dealt with. In chapter one an outline will be given of the historical profile of the Jewish people today. What has made them the way they are, especially with respect to their relations with Christians and the Church? It is impossible to understand any people without some knowledge of their history, and in this chapter it is hoped that needed insights will be learned. Chapter two will examine the different types of Judaism which are to be found today in the Jewish community. Just as it would be quite unhelpful for a Jewish person to lump all Christians together as if they all believed the same about God, worshipped Him in the same manner, and related to the non-Christian world around them in the same way, so it is incorrect to assume that all Jewish people adhere to the same type of Judaism. These first two chapters will set out the contexts for the more specific exploration that is to follow.

In chapter three we will look at the issue of what it means to say that Israel is God's chosen people. What does the Bible say about this? How is the election of Israel into a covenant relationship with God described in the Bible? Is that relationship still in place even though the Church has now come on the scene?

In chapter four we will follow this up with an examination of the issue of the modern restoration of the State of Israel. Is this the fulfilment of the biblical prophecies in which God promised to bring Israel back both to Himself and to sovereign life in the land given to Abraham's descendants?

Chapter five presents an analysis of the awful record of Christian antisemitism, especially as it relates to the common practice of anti-Judaism. Not only have most Christians down the centuries rejected any notion of Jewish restoration to national sovereignty in the land of Israel, but there has been wholesale contempt for the Jewish people altogether. This has led not only to rejection of Judaism, but to the persecution and murder of Jewish people, sometimes actually in the name of Christ.

In chapter six it will be necessary to look at how all of these issues feed into the current debate within the churches, and whether or not there should be any attempt to share the Good News of Jesus with Jewish people. There is a growing lobby, involving Christians within the Roman Catholic Church, within the so-called liberal and pluralist wings of the Protestant churches, and even within the evangelical Protestant churches, to disassociate completely from any sort of Jewish evangelism. Why is this? How should evangelicals respond?

Finally, in chapter seven, we will look at one of the most important matters before us, yet one which is ignored by far too many of the Christian and Jewish scholars and leaders involved in the modern inter-faith dialogue between the two communities. This is the wonderful story of the modern explosion of growth of Jewish Believers in Jesus. There have always been such Jewish Believers, some of whom prefer the name Hebrew Christians, and some of whom, increasingly so today, prefer the name Messianic Jews. As one might imagine, they have always been opposed by the Jewish establishment, but since the 1960s, there has been an amazing growth and development in their numbers and community life. We shall look at this phenomenon and try to see what God is saying to the Church through what He is doing in this community of Jewish people.

This is the reason for a book devoted to the issue of the relationship between the Church and Israel. It is hoped that this will also be the beginning of many readers' own personal search for the answer to the question, 'What is so special about the Jewish people?'

# 1
# Who Are The Jewish People?

It is important at the outset of this work to say something about the present day worldwide community of Jewish people. For many Christians, their personal contact with Jewish people, and their understanding of Judaism, Jewish ethical attitudes, etc, are so poor that they come to Jewish life in a vacuum. But the Jewish world has not existed in a vacuum within the history of humanity, even though the relationship between Jews and non-Jews has been deeply troubled for most of that history. Nor have the Jewish people lived in a time warp since the days of the Bible, as a number of Christians seem to suppose. Theirs is a rich, dynamic and profound history.

The Jewish people whom we meet today, like all other peoples and nations, have been formed partly by their own inner nature and sense of destiny, and partly by their relationship with the peoples among whom they have lived. A number of important perspectives are often brought to bear in this respect by those who are trying to help Christians in the West to appreciate the make-up of the Jewish people. Let us look at these points now.

a) Although there has always been a presence of Jewish people in the land of Israel since the time of Jesus, until 1948 the Jewish story was one of unbroken dispersion among the nations of the world for almost all Jews. It is vital that we appreciate that this was by and large an *enforced exile* from their ancestral and covenantal home. Jewish people longed to return, but were prevented by the host nations among whom they lived. What is more, life for the Jewish communities scattered throughout the world, especially in the Christian countries and regions, was one of poverty, oppression and fear.

b) With few exceptions, this has been a life and history of learning to cope with vulnerability and powerlessness. This kind of existence, endured over many centuries, leaves a mark for some generations to come.

c) This life of exile has meant a need to suppress, or at least subdue, the external expressions of much of Jewish life and religious practice, except in guarded ways within the tight ghetto-like boundaries in which Jewish communities have been forced to live. A contemporary example is the case of the hundreds of thousands of Jewish people from the former Soviet Union who were forbidden to enjoy their Jewish traditions by the government. Until they reached Israel, or until the break-up of the Soviet Union, most had never even been able to see a Bible, let alone celebrate the Passover or circumcise their sons.

d) One of the outcomes of this life of constant pressure and condemnation was the development in the attitudes of many Jews that they needed to prove themselves to the people of the dominant culture. In the face of incessant charges of gross immorality, intellectual and aesthetic inferiority, and the like, many felt the need to do better than would reasonably be required, just to be accepted as all right. An inner drive to excel is therefore inbuilt into many Jewish people, stemming from this attitude of self-defence and community-defence.

e) Another outcome has been a distrust of others, bred down the generations. There is often a general caricature of Jews as hopelessly paranoid, an impression unfortunately reinforced by the work of Jewish artists like Woody Allen. But we must appreciate that the basis of this attitude of distrust of non-Jewish society is quite rational. Jewish people have every reason to doubt the integrity and intentions of their neighbours. This is particularly true when it comes to their Christian neighbours, and so it should come as no surprise to learn that in the Western world Jewish people have often been in the forefront of the political struggle to separate Church and State in the life of a nation. Such a separation is a means of protecting the rights of threatened ethnic and religious minorities.

There is a measure of truth in these points, but on the other hand, we must beware of creating an image of the modern Jewish person as merely a victim. Jewish people have been victimised throughout most of their history since Jesus' time, and much of their reaction against Christian overtures towards them, and against Christian institutions (including the Church itself) is rooted in their repeated experiences in that history. However, the Jewish community has never lost its own inner integrity and sense of destiny. When people begin to look seriously at Jewish achievement, and realise the incredibly disproportionate contribution of Jewish people to all areas of human life (medicine, the arts, the physical and social sciences, human rights campaigning, etc), and when they begin to sense the quality of that Jewish contribution, they also begin to realise that the Jewish community has remained creative, dynamic and philanthropic in spite of all its suffering.

As the Jewish song goes, 'Am Yisrael Hai!' The people of Israel is alive and well! Judaism is not dead either. As we shall see, this in itself has caused a great deal of bitter frustration among Christians who wished that it was dead. But before we look at the present state of the religious faith which we call Judaism, let us take some time to outline the history and pilgrimage of the Jewish people, a story which goes a long way to helping us understand who the Jewish people are today.

## Historical Growth

The six maps at the end of this book give an idea of the geographical spread of the Jewish people throughout history. Map 1 shows the situation at the time of Jesus. The Jewish communities which had been taken into exile by the Assyrians and Babylonians (as we read in the Bible) had taken root in that whole region along the Tigris-Euphrates river basin. The trade routes and the major Greek cities of the eastern Mediterranean Sea had also become attractive to Jewish communities, since they provided open potential for employment, and relatively stable social conditions for anyone prepared to help establish Greek domination. Movement had also begun Westwards into the Latin-speaking lands dominated by Rome.

Map 2 takes us to the time when both Christianity and Judaism were on the verge of establishing their mutually exclusive self-definitions. The Roman Empire was Christianised after the conversion of the Emperor, Constantine, and the Nicene Creed was being drawn up. On the other hand, the Jewish world was moving towards the creation of the Talmud and the normative Rabbinic commentaries on the Hebrew Bible. Jewish communities had settled throughout the Mediterranean world, and had begun to move further west into the whole continent of Europe.

Map 3 presents the situation in the early Middle Ages. Christianity was totally dominant in the Holy Roman Empire. But we must realise that the spread of Jewish communities along North Africa and into Spain had been the result of the rise of Islam as another world power. As we shall see later, the Jewish experience in Islamic lands compared very favourably with that among Christian peoples. The trade routes were still of vital importance for the movement of Jewish families.

Map 4 shows the Jewish world at the time of the Reformation in Europe. By this time, most Jewish people were actually living under Muslim, not Christian, rule. There were two reasons for this: a) The Ottoman Empire, still expanding, offered safe haven for any who chose to align themselves with its Islamic rulers. b) Persecution in the Christian lands of Western Europe was on the increase. In fact a major expression of this antisemitic attitude lay in the forced expulsion of whole Jewish communities. As well as moving south into North Africa and the Mediterranean area, Jews also began to move eastwards into Eastern Europe.

Map 5 takes us to the eve of the 20th century. Trade and the search for safe haven had taken Jewish communities into parts of Southern Africa, Australasia, and North and South America. The really significant area of expansion and growth, however, is that of Eastern Europe. The Enlightenment and Jewish Emancipation had made an irrevocable difference to Jewish life in the West, but it would still take some time before the results would be felt.

Finally, map 6 shows something of the present distribution of Jewish communities throughout the world. Jews fleeing from pogroms in Eastern Europe and from the horrors of the Nazi era in Western Europe moved in large numbers to both Americas in particular. Of course the State of Israel has now become a powerful force in the life of world Jewry.

It is of great importance to realise two fundamental facts about the growth of Jewish communities worldwide: a) Jewish people have been driven by a need to find safe haven and a place where they could be left in peace to live a normal life, just as much, if not more, as by a desire to follow trade routes to ever further regions. b) Jewish life and history has been lived out under two competing religious powers, Christianity and Islam. In our outline of Jewish history which is to come, these different Jewish experiences will be dealt with separately.

## Two Families

We must distinguish between the two families of Jewish life in the world today: the *Ashkenazim* and the *Sepharadim*. Ashkenaz is a Hebrew term for the land we now know as Germany, and the Ashkenazim are those Jewish communities whose modern origins spring from Germany and northern France. The later communities of Scandinavia and Eastern Europe are also in large part descended from this same family of Jews. Their common language outside of the synagogue (where Hebrew was kept alive as the sacred tongue) was formed from a mixture of High German, Hebrew, and other local languages, and is known by the name Yiddish.

Sepharad is a term originally applied to the Iberian peninsula, and the Sepharadim are those Jewish communities which stem from the Jews of Spain and Portugal. At the end of the 15th century they were expelled from the peninsula. Many fled to the Ottoman Empire and the Mediterranean basin, in particular to Turkey, the regions of biblical Israel, North Africa, Greece, Italy and Bulgaria. Significant numbers moved north into Western Europe, settling especially in Holland, Germany and England. The oldest functioning synagogue in Britain, the Bevis Marks synagogue in London, is part of this Spanish-Portugese community's life in England. Eventually, substantial numbers of Sepharadim also travelled to search for peace in North and South America. Their common language, based on Spanish, is called Ladino.

These two families within the Jewish people preserve distinct religious rituals, traditions and customs, as well as their own languages and literature. Occasionally one finds Christians trying to give an analogy by means of the hopelessly inadequate comparison between, say, Anglicans and Baptists. If there is any value to be found in this kind of comparison, then the nearest analogy would in fact be that of the difference between Protestants and the Orthodox churches of the East.

It is possible that in part their differences go back to anthropological changes that came about when the northern tribes of Israel were taken into captivity by the Assyrians in the 8th century BC, whereas the southern tribes of Judah were exiled by the Babylonians in the 6th century BC. The former tribes may therefore have developed (via intermarriage, conversion to Judaism, etc) into the Ashkenazi type, while the latter developed into the Sepharadi type. This is a highly controversial subject among Jewish scholars themselves.

It may also be partly true that differences owe much to the separation of religious authority between the teachers of Israel and Babylon. In the period after the partial restoration under Ezra and Nehemiah, when Jerusalem was rebuilt and community life began afresh in the land of Israel, the population which had settled in those regions of the new Persian Empire remained under the spiritual and cultural leadership of their teachers there. Indeed, in the centuries after the time of Jesus, when the Jewish community was creating its normative code of belief and practice, two distinct Talmuds were formulated. One is known as the Babylonian Talmud, while the other is called the Jerusalem, or Palestinian, Talmud. Perhaps the Ashkenazi communities, because of their geo-political situation, were formed under the aegis of the Palestinian Jewish authorities and customs, a link made credible by the bridge-community of Italian Jewry. This would mean that the Sepharadim owe their development to the dominant influence of Babylon, via the cultural route of North African Jewry.

Whatever the truth of this doubtless complex history, the fact remains that the two families of world Jewry are quite distinct in very many particulars of their faith and practice. Above all, however, it must be stressed that in spite of the real differences between the Ashkenazim and the Sepharadim, they are united as Jews in their devotion to the survival, and indeed the growth of both Judaism as a faith-tradition and the Jewish people as a distinct community.

## Jewish Communities in Muslim Lands

Islamic law decreed that Jews and Christians, known as 'people of the Book' (the Bible), should be accorded a status in Islamic society different from, and superior to that of other religious communities. They were to be protected, and to be given freedom of worship, in return for the payment of certain taxes and an agreement to live under specific restrictions. Within this so-called 'dhimmi status' the Jews managed to live quite well, as a rule. By the time of Muhammad and the rise of Islam, the Jews were already well established in sectors of the Arabian peninsula, including Medina itself. After an initial period of persecution, when Jewish tribes suffered for not accepting the new religion brought by Muhammad, a modus vivendi was worked out.

Things eventually became better for the Jewish people when the Abbasid caliphate, based in Babylonia, arose to rule the Muslim world. Not only was there a form of political stability at last, and a fresh injection of life into the economic markets, but the strongest and most influential Jewish communities were now also in the place of governmental administration. What is more, the Jewish people were allowed to maintain their inner structures— Jewish law courts, rabbinic leadership, etc. The most famous Jewish traveller of the 12th and 13th centuries, Benjamin of Tudela, reported that he found some 40,000 Jews, 28 synagogues, and 10 religious teaching institutes in Baghdad when he visited there. Only a few European Jewish communities could boast this size at the same time in history.

Jewish traders kept moving eastwards from this

base too. From this time we can date the origin of the old Jewish communities in India and China, not to mention Persia and other areas of the so-called Near East. In practice there was a great deal of come-and-go between the Muslim hosts and the Jewish 'guests', although the legislation made it clear that the host-guest distinction was not to be forgotten. Traders, philosophers, and other professionals enjoyed relatively free interaction, with episodes of oppression and intolerance really only happening in isolated and local situations. Of course whenever the Islamic world itself came under substantial threat, as for instance in the 13th century, when the Christian West and the Mongol East both began to make inroads into Muslim territory, then the Jewish people, like all those who were non-Muslims, began to suffer correspondingly.

Nevertheless, we know of no substantial movement of Jewish people from the Muslim world to Europe, largely, no doubt, because the Muslims never expelled Jews from Islamic realms. But traffic the other way was constant, primarily because there was a history of continuous antisemitism in the Christian world. The largest single migration of Jews to Muslim territories followed the expulsion of Jews from the Iberian peninsula from 1492 until 1497. To this day Jewish people still speak favourably of their treatment by Muslims as compared to that by Christians. This point, to the Church's shame, should be noted well.

It is really only the unprecedented conflict over the establishment of the Jewish State of Israel in the

Middle East which has caused the rift between Muslims and Jews in the modern period. It is estimated that perhaps a maximum of 5% of the 900,000 Jews who lived in Muslim countries in 1948, when the State of Israel was declared, still live there. The great majority went, by various routes, to live in Israel. There were two factors leading to this mass exodus: a) Hostility to the Jewish population by the people of the various Muslim countries in which they lived. This aggression was the people's way of protesting against the establishment and on-going life of the State of Israel. b) The positive attraction of Zion to these Jewish communities of the East. Most of them wished to live in their own ancient homeland. The majority of the Israeli population are in fact Sepharadim from the Middle East and North Africa.

Nonetheless, part of the problem of the Middle East for world Jewry is the continued presence of Jewish communities in many of these countries. Fears of reprisals against them for policies or incidents involving Israelis are a constant reality. There are still over 20,000 Jews in both Iran and Turkey; over 10,000 in Morocco; over 1,000 in Syria and Tunisia; and several hundreds in the other countries apart from Lybia. European Christians are often surprised that Jewish people whom they know feel so close to these communities, but, as we have seen, the world of Sepharadi Jewry has extended into Western Europe since the end of the 15th century.

## Jewish Experience in Christian Lands

We can date Christian rule in the world from the early 4th century AD, when Constantine, the Roman Emperor, had some kind of conversion experience and decreed that Christianity should become the official religious faith of the whole Empire. When we think in terms of the formative period of Christian rule over peoples, then we are, of course, thinking about Europe and its history. Other so-called Christian countries (eg the two Americas, Australia and New Zealand) received their faith as a result of the missionary and colonial efforts of Europeans.

From virtually the very beginning, Jewish people and the faith of Judaism suffered persecution at the hands of Christians. There was popular rioting and looting of Jewish homes by the mobs who used anti-Jewish prejudice as a convenient excuse for expressing their economic and social frustrations. But there was also well-organised persecution of Jews by the elite of Europe, which is to say the clergy and the ruling classes. Contempt for Jews as people, and for their spiritual and moral traditions, was taught from pulpit and public platform. Discriminatory legislation was laid down against the Jewish people—for instance, passing the death penalty against any Jewish person who converted a Christian to Judaism, or against a Jew and a Christian who married. Unlike in Islamic countries, the Jewish religious infrastructure was severely curtailed by Christian governments, and confiscation or destruction of buildings and books was not uncommon.

One of the worst episodes in the history of Jewish life in this Christianised Europe took place within the context of the West's crusades against the Muslims who had captured the holy places of Christendom in the so-called Holy Land. Western Christian leaders were convinced that this was an affront to the Gospel, to have the historical-geographical centre of their faith under the control of these enemies of the Gospel. It is a sad fact of history that as well as ideologically-motivated Christian knights and preachers, many thousands of discontented peasants joined the march to Jerusalem in a self-centred search for adventure and wealth. The crowds were easily manipulated by some of the leaders to wage war on the innocent Jewish communities in Europe which they met on their way. The clarion cry went out: 'Why wait till we reach the Holy Land to defeat the enemies of the Gospel when we have the very killers of Christ living here in our midst!' Many thousands of Jews were massacred, and their communities and synagogues razed to the ground in the name of Christ and the Church. The term 'crusade' is still one of the most emotive words in the vocabulary of Jewish-Christian relations.

This whole terrible story of Jewish suffering under Christian rule will be dealt with fully in one of the chapters of the book. One basic factor, though, must be brought out here. Classically, three choices were offered to Jewish people at various times of persecution: death, expulsion and baptism. They might be given the choice of death or conversion/baptism, or the choice of expulsion/confiscation of property or conversion/baptism. At times many thousands of Jewish people actually chose the option of going through the motions of conversion and baptism in order to save their own or their families' lives. Needless to say, this factor has served more than most in embittering the Jewish communities to the phenomenon of Jewish 'conversion'. Fundamentally it is perceived as betraying the memory of the countless Jews who chose the option of death, thus maintaining their spiritual, moral, and personal integrity. As we shall see later, the Jewish community still responds to news of a Jewish person being baptised as a Christian with the assumption that he/she did so for some sort of personal gain.

Another significant outcome of this process of achieving conversions by means of coercion and manipulation was that many Jewish people went through the motions of conversion, but actually kept their Jewish faith intact and dear to them, albeit in secret and in dread of being found out. These 'secret Jews' were called 'marranos', and to this day there are known descendants of those Jews who refused to surrender their faith in the face of Christian oppression. Rather topically, in 1992 we are remembering the voyage of Christopher Columbus from Spain in 1492, the same year as the expulsion of the Jews from Spain. There are still many scholars who believe that Columbus himself was such a marrano.

Protestants are often tempted to practise self-righteousness and blame all of this maltreatment of the Jewish people on the Roman Catholic Church. This Church is held responsible for the evils of so-called Christian Europe in the centuries leading from Constantine to the Reformation. It is certainly true that many Jewish communities were themselves full of praise for the early teaching and practice of Martin Luther. In 1523, for instance, he wrote a hugely controversial and influential tract, entitled, 'That Jesus Christ Was Born A Jew', in which he not only positively stressed the *Jewishness* of Jesus, but blamed the popes and the priests for the reaction of the Jewish people against Jesus. At one point he said:

> If I had been a Jew and had seen such fools and blockheads teach the Christian faith, I should rather have turned into a pig than become a Christian.

Tragically, however, Luther himself gradually became as antisemitic in his attitudes and directions against the Jewish people as anyone before him had been. Perhaps this came about as the result of the resistance (to his Gospel) by the Jews, whom he dearly wished to lead to faith in Jesus. We simply do not know the details of his about-turn, but in 1542, for example, he wrote another tract, entitled, 'On the Jews and Their Lies'. In this, and other similar pieces, he speaks of the Jews as 'venemous and virulent', as 'disgusting vermin', etc. More than this, Luther sometimes recommended expulsion of the Jews, or the burning of their synagogues and sacred books. Countries steeped in Lutheranism have the same type of precedent, then, as those whose roots are Roman Catholic, for contempt of Jews.

Earlier in this chapter it was pointed out that many Jewish people fled to the Muslim world when there was severe persecution in Western Europe. However, many also migrated further eastwards, especially to Poland, which was still part of the Christian world. They met an economic need by providing a form of middle class to serve the feudal aristocracy on the one hand and the peasant workers on the other hand. Centuries of experience in diplomacy, trade and commerce also proved useful to the ruling classes there. But sadly this all came to an end in the terrible pogroms of the mid-17th century, when Cossacks slaughtered something over 100,000 Jews and obliterated some 300 Jewish communities and villages.

Two results of this are worth noting at this stage: a) There was a significant re-migration westwards by many Jewish people who had lost too much in the east to stay there. b) Once again the image of cross-carrying Christian soldiers for Christ was welded in the Jewish consciousness, along with the image of a sword on its way down to kill innocent men, women and children.

Surely this has all changed with the coming of the modern period? We may certainly speak of a radical change in European thinking that came about during the process which we know as the Enlightenment in the 17th and 18th centuries. This is the name given to the intellectual movement which transformed society by challenging the monolithic authority of the Church, and indeed the very concept of received authority or revelation; by the raising up of reason and logic as the basic tools of civilisation; by celebrating mankind's ability to achieve knowledge, and therefore power over himself and the universe; by the rise of the experimental science, whereby the laboratory testing of data became a metaphor for the testing of all truth-claims; in short, by the development of a belief in mankind as a self-endorsing, creative, capable, and organising life of great ability and potential.

In large part this involved a commitment to the separation of Church and State in society, a policy which was one of the basic commitments in the constitution of the United States of America as well. Leaders of the Enlightenment were determined to take the dogma out of society's structures and values, and this meant the overthrow of the Church's domination of the intellectual and cultural life of society. Religious minorities were to be accorded full protection and freedom of expression within the proper parameters of behaviour in a civilised society. As can easily be imagined, this was met with enthusiasm by very many within Jewish society.

Their enthusiasm grew in the 18th and 19th centuries with the period known as Emancipation. This refers to the gradual abolition of restrictions against Jewish people in society, and the granting of religious, civil and political rights to Jewish (as other) people. Jews no longer had to live in ghettoes, to be restricted to certain professions, or to live in a country purely at the discretion of its Christian leadership. Of course there was much residual antipathy to Jewish people, and social acceptance never quite matched the theoretical welcome of the Jewish community into modern Western life. Nevertheless, rights were being accorded to Jews; they were being accepted as citizens of their respective states. The first country to truly emancipate the Jewish people was the USA, at the end of the 18th century.

Before we look at the actual effect this had on Jewish experience in Christian countries, it will be helpful to notice something of its effects on the inner workings and relationships of the Jewish communities themselves. The Jewish communities underwent their own Enlightenment (called the Haskalah, after the Hebrew word for reason) following on about a century after the greater European intellectual revolution. The Jewish leaders of this movement believed that Jews suffered chiefly because they were so different from, so out of step with, their host cultures in terms of language, customs, dress, education, etc. In step with the gradual opening up of the western powers to the granting of citizenship and basic human rights to Jewish people, the Jewish Enlightenment sought to help Jewry break out of the ghetto once and for all.

Physically and socially this involved a literal movement out of the ghettoes; Jews developed social mobility to various degrees, depending on the particular national or regional situation. This led to a considerable degree of assimilation to non-Jewish standards and life-styles, with increasing numbers of Jews marrying non-Jews. Many Jewish people converted to Christianity in order to better themselves in the host country's Christian culture, which, in spite of what the legislation might say, was still biased against Jews and Judaism. Among specific changes which were advocated and indeed practised within the Jewish community were the following: the adding of 'secular' subjects to the traditional Talmud-based curriculum of Jewish schools; learning and using the local vernacular language; dressing in the modern European styles; reforming the synagogue services; and getting involved in new occupations.

An example of one of the revolutionary outcomes of the Haskalah was the translation of the five Books of Moses into German by Moses Mendelssohn, an act which caused massive consternation among the traditional Orthodox communities within Jewry. As a matter of fact, the Orthodox establishment decried the whole movement from the beginning. This was partly because of their fear (rationally based as it turned out) that it would lead to wholesale assimilation by large sections of the Jewish population, burdened over so many generations by repression and oppression at the hands of those who were now offering liberation. It was also partly in reaction to the commitment of these reformers to the de-dogmatising of Judaism; to the triumph of reason over established authority and tradition; to the attempt to make the Jewish faith contextually suited to life in a new and cosmopolitan Europe.

In other words, both the established Church and Synagogue authorities were deeply disturbed by the Enlightenment. As we have noted already, social opinion was still out of step with the enlightened legislation of the intellectual and political leaders of the new world. Jewish people still faced a wall of prejudice when they tried to take the new order at its word and live as equal citizens. The exception to this, as a rule, was the situation in the USA, where Jewish immigrants and religious refugees rubbed shoulders with other ethnic and religious groups from the very beginning. Generally speaking, however, the historical trend towards real equality seemed to many Jews to be irrevocable, in spite of local setbacks when reactionary forces indulged in continuing antisemitic attitudes and activities.

Then came the 1880s. Czar Alexander II was assassinated in 1881 and the Jews of Russia were blamed. There followed nine months or so of horrific pogroms, carried out with the covert blessing of officialdom. In May 1882 the infamous May Laws were passed, reversing all the recent reforms in Russia and subjecting the Jewish people once more to inhuman treatment. At the same time an avowedly antisemitic political party in Germany won some seats in the government there, and Hungary saw the rise of a new wave of antisemitism. The same story began to unfold in other countries; anti-Jewish literature was spread abroad in great quantities and antisemitic societies were formed. The Jewish community suffered legal, verbal and physical violence, and once again fear began to dominate Jewish thinking and living.

As we come, then, to the eve of our own time, there are two outcomes of this turbulent century which we must note. First of all, there was yet again a massive movement of Jewish people from the east of Europe to the west. Of course the 19th century was an era of huge population movements both within and from Europe, and Jewish people fitted into this overall picture. They migrated not only to Western Europe (including Britain, where by the time of the First World War over 80% of the Jewish people were from the immigrant population), but also to the Americas, South Africa and Australasia. It is therefore from the end of the 19th century that many date the rise of Jewish communities throughout the contemporary world. It also helps to explain, for instance, why the Jewish community of Britain was so antagonistic to the proposed Bill to restrict immigration which was being considered by the British government in 1991-2. Very few British Jewish families would be able to react in a way other than to say to themselves that if such a law had existed in generations past then their forefathers would all have perished in Europe. Britain's Jewish community is largely descended from such immigrants.

The second thing to note is that this is the context in which to see the rise of the modern political Zionist movement. Theodore Herzl, the founder of this movement for Jewish national liberation, was a very assimilated Viennese Jewish journalist who looked forward to a civilised life for himself and all Jews in the new Europe. However, his life was changed while he was covering the notorious Dreyfus Trial in France in 1894. Captain Alfred Dreyfus was a French Jewish officer who was scandalously made a scapegoat for an act of treason. Herzl's own coverage of the mockery of a trial, and the French public's willingness to lap it up, managed to convince him that contrary to his hopes and beliefs, there was in fact no hope for the Jewish people to be accepted as equal citizens and full human beings in the countries which tolerated them within their borders. He became convinced of the need for a Jewish homeland that would be their own country, with their own government and society, and with the ability to defend themselves, if need be, against their enemies. In short, Zionism was born in the context of intransigent antisemitism within Christian European society.

The issues of Zionism and Christian responses to it will be dealt with fully in one of the chapters of this book, but perhaps enough has been said here to help Christians appreciate more the deeply felt commitment that Jewish people the world over have to this one Jewish State. It is an anchor in the sea of fear and turmoil; it is a haven of safety for any Jews who come up against hostile actions on behalf of governments or societies throughout the world; it is a symbol of Jewish life and the possibility of peace to come; it represents Jewish victory against all the odds of history.

There is one more aspect of modern Jewish life which must be mentioned before we can be in a position of understanding what makes today's Jewish person the person he/she is. This is, of course, the terrible event known as the Holocaust. Again, this will be dealt with in the chapter on antisemitism, but it must be singled out in this historical outline as well, since it is one of the determinants of contemporary Jewish life. Although one can look back in retrospect and see the signs, the fact is that there was no-one who was prepared for the Nazi policy of the complete eradication of the Jewish people from the face of Europe (and eventually from the whole earth, had Hitler managed to conquer it).

Several factors led to the rise of National Socialism in Germany in the 1930s. The same mixture of historical, social, economic and political factors also aggravated and built upon the hatred of the Jews. This was to culminate in the policy and the attempted practice of not only murdering all Jews and people with Jewish blood in their family lines, but also of totally obliterating all signs of Jewish life, except for a museum where relics would be kept for the purposes of propagating the Nazi revisionist version of history. However, we must realise that none of the treatment of the Jews, either from the active perpetrators of torture and extermination, or from the point of view of the passive citizens who were accessories before, during and after the fact—would have been possible apart from the centuries of contempt for, and abuse of, the Jews, which had become part and parcel of the ideological fabric of Christendom.

Perhaps, not surprisingly, many Jewish people see the establishment of the State of Israel in 1948 as a miracle. Who could have foreseen, less than a decade earlier, when the Jewish population of Europe was undergoing an experience of complete destruction, that within three years of the end of the war there would be not only a surviving Jewish people, but also an actual sovereign Jewish State? Some have even described this as an experience of crucifixion and resurrection!

In this chapter I have tried to provide some idea of the Jewish experience in history. No people have ever suffered at the hands of Christians to anything like the extent that the Jewish people have. Therefore no Christian can afford to be ignorant of this history, especially if he/she wishes to understand the typical Jewish reactions to the Christian preaching of the Gospel. There is a lot of truth in the old adage that people judge Jesus by the Christians they meet.

# 2

# Is Judaism The Same For All Jews?

Far too many Christians assume that Jewish people think and believe today exactly as they did at the time of Jesus. Nothing could be further from the truth.

Even at that time there was a great and rich diversity of religious belief and practice. Familiarity with the New Testament brings with it an awareness of the Pharisees and the Sadducees, two quite different, and in some ways, conflicting religious communities. But there was also the community of extremely strict Essenes, generally held to be the people responsible for the Dead Sea Scrolls found at Qumran. Quite apart from anything else, they rejected the authority of the priesthood in Jerusalem and everything which went on in the temple there. Then there were various groupings of Jewish people who had in common an apocalyptic sense that God was about to intervene dramatically in history and overthrow Roman power in a cataclysmic war. These

Jews were to be found in some numbers, especially in the Galilee region, and they are the groups usually referred to as Zealots. After the coming of Jesus, there was also the rapidly growing movement of Messianic Jews, those who followed Jesus as the promised Messiah of Israel.

The Christian West is used to calling the time of Jesus the age of 'late Judaism', reflecting its own sense of having superseded Israel as the true people of God. Judaism is assigned to the failures of past history in the light of the coming of Jesus to fulfil all that Israel was meant to be. Therefore it is referred to as 'late' Judaism, suggesting that it was on its last legs. In actual fact, Judaism and Christianity, as they have developed, are *both* daughters of the faith of Israel in the generations before the birth of Jesus. Both claim to be the only authentic daughter, of course, each accusing the other of being an imposter. At the moment, however, my point is simply this: properly speaking, the time of Jesus and the growth of the early church is the age of 'early Judaism' too. It was a creative and dynamic period for Judaism as well as for Christianity. Christians must beware of lumping all Jewish people together in the days of Jesus, as if they all thought the same about God and the way He acts in people's lives.

Our concern in this book is the contemporary scene vis-a-vis the nature of Judaism and the Jewish people, but one more point must be made about the situation in the opening generations of the Christian era, if we are to understand the way that the various strands of Judaism have come to be the way they are. Jewish culture is saturated with religious thought and symbolism, and it is true to say that the over-whelmingly dominant influence on Jewish society and culture today has been what we now know as Orthodox Judaism. The origins of this dominant Judaism go back to the period after the Romans destroyed the temple in Jerusalem, in 70 AD. The very term 'rabbi' dates from this time. Before this, when the temple still stood, the Jewish people had the variety of religious options outlined above. However, when the temple was destroyed, the Sadducees lost their base of power, as they were the priestly class par excellence. Sixty years or more later, the Romans wiped out the last real vestige of Jewish resistance, when they manoeuvered the Jewish fighters and their families to the Dead Sea area of Masada. As is well known, these Jews chose a death by community suicide. The Essenes and the various Zealot groups were therefore effectively silenced.

In short, the only group which survived with its basic religious outlook intact was the community of Pharisees (a lay group, not, as many Christians suppose, a priestly or professional religious group). The rabbis whom we know from the Talmud, and down Jewish history, are the spiritual and political heirs of the Pharisees. Because of the loss of the temple, and therefore of any religion which was sacrificially-based, the practice of Judaism had to change, if only for the interim period until the temple could be rebuilt. In fact Orthodox Judaism still considers the present state of affairs in which there is no Jerusalem temple as a *theological* interim (although it has lasted almost 2,000 years) which will be put right when the Messiah comes. In this temple-less life, the rabbis proposed that the Jewish faith be centred on four religious attitudes and practices, and they remain as the typical Jewish focuses: Torah, prayer, repentance and charity.

What is no longer typical in the Jewish world is a traditional commitment to Orthodox Judaism. Most Jewish people today are not Orthodox, at least not in a way which would be acceptable to Orthodoxy's leadership. The development of the modern shape of Jewish religious life is really a series of reactions and counter-reactions to the Orthodoxy which had so dominated the Jewish world. We only have space here to mention some of the most fundamental developments, those which are indispensible for any understanding of the Jewish faith-communities today.

## The Hasidic Movement

The Christian image of a typical Jewish person is based on the followers of this particular movement, in which the men are classically dressed in long black clothes, with long beards, and long earlocks of hair. The Hasidic revolution occurred in 18th century Poland, but grew in influence over the next century and more throughout the Jewish world. The people are called Hasidim, from the Hebrew word for 'pious people'. Although they are very strictly Orthodox, their eruption into the world of Jewry was traumatic, to say the least. Several factors led to the rise of this movement:

a) Eastern European Jewry in particular was still in deep shock and depression following the pogroms and deterioration in life which came with the Cossack rising in the mid-17th century. The Jewish masses were ready for some type of more mystical religious faith, one which would give them a new sense of God's presence and of His promise of a fulfilled future.

b) Related to the first point, the late 17th century had also seen the rise and fall of Shabbetai Tzvi, a Jewish man who had claimed to be Israel's promised Messiah. Great numbers of Jews believed this (as many did even after his ignominious death as a convert to Islam), and the bitter disappointment of yet another false Messiah also made the Jewish people ready for a fresh way of experiencing the reality of God in their lives.

c) Underlying all this was a growing dissatisfaction with the status quo of Orthodox Jewish spirituality, which to large numbers of simple Jews was inaccessibly intellectual. It did not meet the need for an existential (one might even say intimate) relationship with God. People wanted something more warm, more satisfying, more immediate.

The founder of Hasidism, known as the Baal Shem Tov (meaning the Master of the Good Name), taught that personal devotion, sincere prayers, and a joyful relationship with God were more acceptable to God than great intellectual learning. His movement caught up huge numbers of Jewish people, though in a fashion not unfamiliar to Protestant Christians, there soon developed divergent Hasidic groups, each led by its own spiritual Tzaddik, or Righteous Man. Many Christian pilgrims to Israel will have seen large groups of these black-coated Hasidim singing and dancing enthusiastically at the Western Wall in Jerusalem. Occasionally one will see a car in Britain with a sticker which proclaims, 'We want Messiah now!' The Jewish people who share this kind of Messianic fervour are also descendants of this Hasidic movement within modern Jewry.

There were, and are, opponents of this movement within Orthodox Judaism; certain Talmudists feared that Hasidic enthusiasm would lead to the unwitting violation of basic religious precepts. In the early years of this conflict within Jewry, it would not be an exaggeration to say that the opponents actively persecuted followers of the various Hasidic groups.

## The Reform Movement

Both the Hasidim and their opponents, however, united to some extent in their common hostility to another branch of Judaism which developed under the influence of the Enlightenment, which we spoke about in the previous chapter. The so-called Reform movement arose early in the 19th century as a commitment to adapt and explain the ritual and basic religious concepts of Judaism for life in the new, rationalistic and liberal West. Orthodox Jews condemned it out of hand as simply pandering to the irreligious spirit of the age; a betrayal of the timeless truths of Jewish faith and practice; a barely concealed half-way house to complete assimilation into non-Jewish culture and thought.

The leaders of Reform saw it differently, of course. They were determined to produce a form of Jewish faith suitable to the principle that one's religion should stay at home, it is true, but they wanted it to be nonetheless a vibrant faith for its practitioners. They also saw it as an advance to rid the synagogue services and other traditional practices of what were interpreted as archaisms for the sake of it. Judaism had to be seen as a religion for the present age, not just for ages gone by. Not only this, but they went a step further in proclaiming that Jews were not a nation, properly speaking, but people of a particular religious persuasion. Jews should be loyal citizens of their adoptive countries. This actually led to the early Reformers opposing the Zionist movement when it began, although in more recent times the Reform movement has become fully committed to the State of Israel and the Zionist cause. This issue of Jewish responses to the Zionist movement will be specifically dealt with in a later chapter.

Many Christians today will have found Reform Jews to be more accessible than Orthodox Jews, and may even have visited Reform synagogues or attended Jewish-Christian dialogues where it is normally Reform rabbis or lay-people who represent the Jewish point of view. Some of the factors which distinguish Reform worship from Orthodox synagogue services are the mixed seating of men and women; the use of the vernacular language as well as Hebrew; the use of organs and pianos; and the full role of women at every level of leadership, including that of rabbi. Traditional Jewish sources, like the Talmud, are given respect, but they are not regarded as being an unalterable or unquestionable body of divine revelation, as they are by the Orthodox.

Considerable enmity exists between the Orthodox and the Reform communities at various points. Christians are often heard to say that they have more in common with the Reform community, since that community is open to, and indeed heavily involved in, inter-faith dialogue at local as well as scholarly levels. It is also responding to the same problems of secular modernity and pluralism in the way that many Christians are. Some Christians also like the fact that Reform Judaism is not preoccupied with the Law and tradition, and so feel freer to share openly about the ethical and social issues which are facing us all today.

On the other hand, there are Christians who maintain that the Reformers gave up too much to the secular humanism which came out of the Enlightenment, just like the so-called 'liberals' within the Church. These Christians feel much closer to Orthodox Jews in that they both preserve their faith in the supernatural God of the Bible; they both believe the Bible (not the New Testament in the case of Jews, of course) to be the very revelation of God's will; and they both look forward to the Messianic Age when God will bring to fulfilment all His purposes for the world. The differences between them are still great, but nevertheless the basic worldview is similar, and they can understand one another's frame of reference.

## The Ultra-Orthodox

This is a term which is often used quite loosely by Christians and Jews alike, but there was a distinct development in the early 19th century of what is usually known by this name. The confrontation between those who advocated reform and those who held on for the status quo was most bitter in Hungary, from where fierce exchanges moved out into other parts of Eastern Europe. One of the founders of this anti-reform movement, Rabbi Moses Sofer, made it clear in his teaching that all innovation in Jewish religious life and practice was without doubt a violation of God's will for the Jewish people. Followers of this rabbi and his many disciples began to set themselves apart physically as well as theologically from the rest of Jewry—even from the other Orthodox Jewish communities. Descendants from these ultra-Orthodox groups maintain a distinct community presence in Israel, the USA, and other parts of the world, including Britain.

## Neo-Orthodoxy

Not all reaction to the innovations of the reformers was as extreme as that of the ultra-Orthodox. Especially in Germany and Italy in the mid-19th century, there was a significant development by Jewish leaders who sought to wed something of the possibilities of modern Jewish interaction with the best of non-Jewish culture and the basic tenets and practices of traditional Judaism (for instance the concept of the Written Torah and the Oral Torah as both being revelation from God). Followers of this movement paraded the motto, 'Torah im derech eretz', a saying which means something like, 'Our revealed religion, but also the host culture's own wisdom'.

At the start of the 20th century this form of Orthodoxy, which is also committed to receiving the best from the scientific, educational insights and practices of the non-Jewish world, began to take root in the USA, where it flourishes to this very day. A significant development has been the combination of traditional Talmudic and other studies with a modern university education in special institutions of higher learning. Their claim is to have achieved the integration of Jewish and non-Jewish life which remains faithful, first and foremost, to the revealed religion, but also interacts with the larger world in meaningful ways.

## The Conservative Movement

This movement arose in the mid-19th century as yet another response to the challenge of modernism. There were Jews in Germany who were as dissatisfied as any with the tradition-bound services and customs of the Orthodox, and yet who also rejected the full-blown reaction of the reformers as having surrendered too much to the spirit of the times. Sometimes the leaders of this movement are presented as people who wanted change to come about in the Jewish community as a result of evolutionary, not revolutionary, processes. They were positively disposed to the traditional laws and practices, but also accepted that Judaism was a religion which itself was in a process of historical change and development. They wanted to identify openly with the value of, and indeed the need for, change. In short, they saw themselves, as they still do, as the 'conservers' of Jewish faith and culture in the modern age.

As examples of the beliefs and practices of the Conservatives, we may mention the following: the separate seating of men and women in synagogue; an acceptance of the need for some Jewish people to have to drive to synagogue on the Sabbath; the ordination of women as rabbis and the training of women as cantors; the belief that the Torah is authoritative, but not the actual word of God, with a commitment to using the principles which can be inferred from the Talmud in settling ethical and practical issues, rather than a slavish adherence to the decisions and practices of previous leaders and generations.

It was in the USA that the Conservative movement really took root and began to thrive. It is still an extremely powerful movement there, and is expanding in appeal in many other parts of the world, especially in South America, Israel and Britain. Outside of the USA it generally chooses to be known as the Masorti movement, this being a Hebrew term meaning 'traditional'. However it is not nearly traditional enough for the Orthodox, who regard it as simply a disguised form of Reform Judaism. On the other hand, Reform Judaism sees it as too traditional, trying to win the reluctant blessing of the Orthodox. As yet, Christians in Britain have had very little exposure to Masorti Judaism, but there is no doubt that it is a movement with a growing appeal to Jews who are themselves dissatisfied with the (middle-of-the-road-Orthodox) United Synagogue and also the (Liberal or Reform) Progressive movement.

## The Reconstructionist Movement

In a sense this is only relevant to an examination of Judaism in the USA, because it is almost entirely limited in its membership to American Jewry. But paradoxically, especially in light of the fact that its numerical strength world-wide is also fairly limited, the basic perspective and drive of Reconstructionism has had an influence on western Jewry out of all proportion to its size. Interestingly, it is really the creation of one man, Rabbi Mordecai Kaplan, who was himself a member of the Conservative movement in the USA until he broke with it in the 1920s. This is, then, a very young movement. In fact Kaplan originally perceived his role (and that of his followers) as that of an enabler, one who would help the various Jewish religious parties to see the truths of his insights and convictions, rather than as the founder of yet another Jewish movement.

Kaplan appreciated the role of the Reform movement in forcing the issue of the need to adapt Judaism to the developing world, but he rejected its low opinion of ritual, and especially the fact that it stripped the Jewish people of nationhood. However he was in conflict with the Orthodox on too many issues to support them. He rejected the idea of a supernatural God, and denied that the Torah was a literal revelation from God. Conservative Judaism was criticised for lacking the courage of its latent convictions in reforming or altering the laws of Judaism, although he praised its commitment to the primacy of the Jewish people and to Jewish culture. Kaplan also had a major challenge to the Zionists in that he said they had no properly developed and integrated idea of the Jewish people as a whole, Diaspora as well as Israel.

What Kaplan and his disciples have maintained, therefore, is that Judaism is in need of a thorough reconstruction of its definition of itself, and of its way of life in the modern world. Jewish people must learn to live in two civilisations at the same time, borrowing from each and simultaneously enriching each. Judaism is presented as an amalgam of religion, history, culture, customs, language, etc. In fact it is a whole civilisation, and moreover it is one which has been evolving over the generations. It must also be stressed that the Reconstuctionists are insistent that it is a *religious* civilisation.

Even though the numbers of paid-up members of this movement are relatively small (certainly outside of the USA), the notion that the key concept in Judaism is that of Jewish peoplehood, or Jewish civilisation, has gained great acceptance among masses of Jewish people. It makes no demands for a supernaturalist worldview; it has no role for obedience to a supposedly revealed body of literature; and it allows the maximum of interaction with the non-Jewish world around. Many modern Jewish people who might be termed by Christians as 'secularised' in fact believe that in a sense their very Jewishness and love of Jewish culture is an acceptable form of religious expression. In this they are following the confident lead of Kaplan and his school of thought.

This has been a brief outline of the history which has made Jewish people who they are today. This is something of the story of the Jewish people who live' next door to the Christians who will read this book. The specific issues taken up in the following chapters now have some context. In a sense the obvious question to come out of this history is this: 'Who, then, is a Jew?' The answer to the question involves matters of race, nationality and religion. It is much easier to define a Celt, or a British citizen, or a Christian, since although one can be any combination of the three, they are each quite distinct. Somehow all three of these matters are mixed up when we consider what being a Jew entails.

In the final chapter of the book we shall investigate the claim of Jewish people who come to faith in Jesus as Israel's Messiah, that they are also still Jewish, and in fact more authentically Jewish than before their new-found faith. This claim is roundly rejected by the various Jewish establishments, who counter-claim that such Jewish people are apostates and traitors to the Jewish people and to Judaism. We must ask ourselves what right have non-Jewish Christians to contribute to this debate between Messianic Jews and other Jewish people? What answer will non-Jewish Christians give to the question—are Jewish believers in Jesus to be supported by the Church as still being Jewish?

This issue of Jewish identity, defined not simply as the identity of any given individual Jewish person, but more importantly, as the identity of the Jewish community, is really the fundamental one which Christians *as Christians* have to face. Where does God come into it all? Do we find the true definition of who is a Jew when we look in the Bible? Is a relationship with Jesus necessary in order for someone to be a truly authentic Jew?

Or to put it another way, the question often asked by Christians is, in the words of the sub title of our book: 'What is so special about the Jews?'

# 3
# How Long Does God's Choice Last?

What usually happens when Christians begin to discuss the Jewish people and their part in God's plans for the redemption of the world, is that focus is placed on the various restoration prophecies concerning the life of Israel in 'the end times'. People then debate whether or not the modern State of Israel is, or could be, the fulfilment of those biblical promises. This is all very important, and we shall look at the issues involved in the next chapter, but it is not the fundamental issue which should concern the Church in the matter of the relationship between both communities in the purposes of God.

## God's Chosen People

The most important issue by far is the significance and nature of the call of Israel by God. The election of Israel, and the nature of her relationship with God, are the two sides of the coin which must con-

57

cern us most as we seek to understand the relationship between the Jewish people and the Church, which also sees itself as uniquely called by God into a covenant relationship with Himself. At the very least it must be said that since it is the one God who chose both the people of Israel and the Church, and since the Bible clearly shows us that God is consistent with Himself, then contrary to the teaching of much Christian tradition, the election and destiny of the Church cannot contradict that of Israel. In this chapter, therefore, we shall take a careful look at the election of Israel by God.

Christians often think of the phrase, 'the chosen people' when asked about associations with Israel, but the biblical reality behind this phrase is largely unexplored. Not only that, but the possibility that the Jewish people of today might be living heirs of that 'chosenness' has been ignored or rejected by most Christians. As we shall see in a later chapter, there have always been Christians whose reading of the Bible convinced them of God's continuing purpose for His 'ancient people', but they have always been a minority, sometimes marginalised by the mainstream church leaderships. It will therefore be necessary right at the start of this short study to highlight the biblical teaching about God's election of Israel.

There is a basic need in our human nature to be needed, to be considered valuable, important, or special, even if only to one person. Babies and children who grow up with a healthy amount of attention, praise, care and respect become mature adults, able to relate well to others. But those who grow up with

constant criticism, with a feeling of only being tolerated, or with a lack of personal love and praise, such
people become lonely, joyless, and often unable to
accept genuine love and respect—even from God
Himself! The truth is that each person *is* loved and
valued personally by God. We are all created in His
image, and He wishes each of us to be given this love
and respect from one another. In the Bible we constantly read that God demands that we treat one
another in this way. Part of the origin of this basic
need is to be found in the way God made us, and is
consequently right and proper.

However there is another source which feeds into
this desire to be special, namely our self-centredness,
arising from our fallen human nature. Part of us
wants to be in control, to be secure, to be satisfied,
even at the expense of others, to be able to say, to
ourselves at least, that we are better than others.
Unfortunately, these two dimensions of our nature
are completely mixed up within us, so that it
becomes very difficult to trust that our motives or
feelings are really godly.

All of this applies on the level of societies, groups
and nations as well. Competitiveness, ambition,
snobbery, and prejudice all reflect the selfish desire
to be top. And we are aware of the terrible consequences which follow when people are free to act in
accordance with a sense of their own superiority.
Christians therefore are naturally suspicious of any
such claims to specialness, whether they are made by
individuals (like the leaders of so many cults), groups
(like some Christian sects), or nations (like the

plethora of oppressive nationalisms which have arisen throughout history).

Yet Christians claim this very privilege for themselves! We claim to be God's people, the temple of the Holy Spirit, the Body of Christ on earth and the household of faith. This is the Church's understanding of herself in the light of her reading of Scripture, and of her own experience. Thus we can perhaps begin to grasp why it is that the Church has always been particularly keen to repudiate the Jewish claim that they are still the chosen people of God. When Jewish people claim this, they call into question, in a unique way, the self-same claim of the Church. Both Jews and Christians base themselves on the same texts from the Hebrew Bible; they both base their claims on a relationship with the God of Abraham, Isaac, and Jacob; and they both claim the right to be seen as God's witnesses in history. The Church has responded by declaring that the Jewish people are no longer the Israel of God; they have forfeited any claims to being the chosen people by rejecting God's offer of the New Covenant in Jesus. In fact, not only are they now therefore clinging on to an old covenant, but since that covenant is no longer operative, they effectively have *no* covenant relationship with God at all.

This is the heart of what has come to be known as the Church's doctrine of 'supersessionism'—the Church has superseded Israel as the chosen people of God. In other words, some Christians teach that the Church has replaced Israel altogether in God's love and purposes, leaving no place at all for Israel, which is rejected by God. Yet it cannot be as simple as that.

If we turn again to the passage in Romans 9:4–5 we see that Paul is conscious of Israel's continuing place in God's love and plans. And what of Romans 11:29, where Paul states that Israel's special relationship with God cannot be broken, since 'God's gifts and his call are irrevocable'? Here then is our dilemma: if it is true that the Jewish people are still in a special relationship with God through God's commitment to Abraham, and if it is true that Christians are also in a special relationship with God through the life and death of Jesus, what is the nature of the relationship between the two special communities? This in fact is the nub of the matter.

## The Election of Israel

To begin to answer that question we must proceed from a study of the biblical material concerning the call and covenant relationship of Israel. What do we mean when we talk about the 'election' of Israel? Here is a working definition of the theological term election:

> The act of choice whereby God picks an individual
> or group out of a larger company for the purpose or
> destiny of his own appointment.

The election of Abram, and in him the election of Israel, is thus God's choice of Israel out of all the peoples of the world, all of whom He created and loves, for a purpose which involves the ultimate blessing of all those nations (Gen 12:1–3). What is the basis of this choice of Israel? Simply God's own sovereign love and grace (Deut 7:7; 23:5). It was not based on any inherent quality or power within the people, as Christians are so often happy to point out, but nor was it based upon some form of works-righteousness or legalism, as Christians are sometimes wont to fancy. When Paul spoke about this issue in Romans 9—11, he was amazed at the grace of God in His choice of Israel, and concluded those great chapters with a doxology:

> Oh, the depth of the riches of the wisdom and know-ledge of God! How unsearchable his judgements, and his paths beyond tracing out! (Rom 11:33).

What then is the purpose of the election of Israel? It is certainly not so that Israel could enjoy a life of splendid isolation with her God, relishing all the blessings and privileges of her honourable status. She *will* receive the special protection and blessing of God which comes from being His chosen people (Gen 12:2), but that is not the purpose of the choice. It is also true to say that there is a sense in which Israel's duty and responsibility as the people of God is to worship and serve Him in the way that befits His glory and holiness, as distinct from the nations, who worship other gods and follow other lifestyles (Deut 6:1–9). However, the point of Israel's election goes way beyond this. God loves all His peoples, and intends to bring blessing to them all, and so Israel's task is to be the channel whereby God can bless the world. This is a vital aspect of the call of Abraham, as we see in Genesis 12:3, in which God says:

> I will bless those who bless you, and whoever curses

you I will curse; and all peoples on earth will be blessed through you.

Isaiah says this clearly to Israel when he proclaims God's word:

I will keep you and make you to be a covenant for the people and a light for the Gentiles (Is 42:6).

In other words, Israel became an instrument of God's own missionary zeal for the world, and was chosen for that special purpose. (The same must be said about the Church—Christians are also caught up in this same missionary zeal and purpose of God, reaching out to the world, not resting selfishly in their own salvation.) We are talking about a special relationship between God and Israel, a relationship which is summed up in the recurring words of God in the Bible, 'I will be your God and you will be my people'. This relationship is called a 'covenant' in the Bible, so we must look now at what the Bible teaches us about Israel's covenant relationship with the Lord.

## God's Covenant With Israel

A covenant is a special type of relationship in which two parties enter into an alliance which involves a firm commitment to one another, and which usually makes demands on each party. It can be between two individuals (eg in the Bible we see one between David and Jonathan, 1 Sam 18:1–4), but covenants are classically between nations or other powerful groups. At the international level, although there are covenants between equal parties, they usually involve an alliance between two unequal parties, the stronger one pledging protection and help to the weaker in return for some form of vassal status. This' is the pattern followed in the biblical picture of God's relationship with Israel. It is always made clear that the initiative is God's, that He makes covenants with His people, not vice versa, and that He is the superior party in the covenant. God promises His protection and His commitment to Israel, in return for which she must pledge herself to worshipping and serving Him alone, living in conformity with His moral and social standards.

Does this mean that God's covenant, as we find it in the Bible, is therefore conditional? There are certainly obligations laid upon Israel: She must worship the Lord alone; she must be loyal to Him in every sphere of life; she must be His witness to all the nations. However, at heart, the covenants are not *based* on Israel's response to God, even though that is not only expected, but also demanded. They are based fully and squarely on God's gracious and sovereign choice of Israel. (The very same is true, of course, of the relationship between every Christian and God. There are demands made upon Christians, and upon the Church as a whole, which involve the worship of God and one's total life and behaviour, but they are not the basis of the relationship.)

This point will be stressed throughout the present chapter, because Christians traditionally delight in keeping alive the false stereotype that Israel's relationship with God in the Old Testament was conditional on a life of complete righteousness vis-a-vis the Law. This is then contrasted with the relationship between Christians and God in the New Testament, which is said to be independent of the life and will of the Christian, and based totally on the love of God. In fact the truth is that both Testaments present the same picture of covenant relationship with God; it is *always based on God's prior grace and will*, and it *always makes demands on the people involved* in terms of how they must live their lives now that they are in a relationship with the God of Abraham, Isaac and Jacob. Israel's relationship with God is based on the grace of God, as we shall see in this chapter; there are many obligations on Christians to be found in the New Testament, and many passages like the following:

> If you love me, you will obey what I command...You are my friends if you do what I command...faith without deeds is dead...This is how we know that we love the children of God: by loving God and carrying out his commands (Jn 14:15; 15:14; Jas 2:26; 1 Jn 5:2).

It is therefore of fundamental importance for us to realise that God's covenants with His people are never, strictly speaking, conditional. God makes it clear that He will remove His blessings if Israel is disobedient to Him (eg Deut 28:15–19), but He will never reject Israel or withdraw His loving commitment to her (as we see, for example, in Is 49:15f; Hos 11:8–9). God will punish, certainly, but He will do so as a result of His love for Israel, not because He is abandoning her. People often make the mistake of contrasting a God who punishes with a God who forgives, as if the God of Israel is less loving and forgiving than the God of the New Testament. Let's look at one of the key passages in the Hebrew Bible which speaks about God's punishment of Israel as in fact coming from His love for her:

> My son, do not despise the Lord's discipline and do not resent his rebuke, because the Lord disciplines those he loves, as a father the son he delights in (Prov 2:11f).

This is the correct model to use when trying to understand the biblical picture—it is analogous to the way in which any loving and proud parent will know the need to punish a child in order to train and discipline that child. In other words, the contrast is not between someone who punishes and someone who forgives, but between someone who cares enough to punish and discipline, and someone who cares so little that he/she is prepared to leave a child to his/her own devices. When we see God removing His blessings to Israel, it is not a sign of His rejection, but in fact of the opposite!

God's promise of an *everlasting* covenant relationship with Israel is clearly presented in several passages (eg Gen 17:19; Jer 31:35–37; Rom 11:29). Let us look for a moment at the five principal covenants in the Bible.

1. *The covenant with Noah.* Some Christians speak of a covenant with Adam as being the first in the Bible, but the Bible itself never uses this term with respect to Adam. Creation was certainly an act of God's love and initiative, and it shows His fundamental commitment to all of humanity. However, the first example of a covenant is the one made with Noah. In spite of the terrible way in which people had corrupted their lives and their societies (Gen 6:5–6), God renewed His commitment to humanity through the choice of Noah and his family:

But I will establish my covenant with you... (Gen 6:18).

All of life is therefore saved by this pre-flood covenant. The obligation which came to Noah, and which followed on from God's election of Noah, was to be obedient in building the ark, an obedience which was in turn dependent on his trusting relationship with God. After the flood God's pledge was renewed:

I now establish my covenant with you... (Gen 9:9).

Even though Genesis 9:4–6 sets out some definitions and limitations, no actual conditions are mentioned for the establishing of the covenant, and indeed the regular breaking of this boundary-setting does not bring about the abrogation of the covenant (cf the pre- and post-flood comments in Gen 6:5 and Gen 8:21). The very sign of the covenant, the rainbow, symbolises it as God's transcendent commitment and responsibility as regards all of humanity (Gen 9:12–17). Just as the rainbow is independent of humanity's efforts and behaviour, so too is the gracious act of God in initiating and continuing the covenant.

2. *The covenant with Abram/Abraham.* Here we also see that this covenant is grounded in God's gracious choice of Abram, involving him in a future not of his own choosing (Gen 12:1). God's commitment within the relationship is expressed in the promise of land (Gen 15:18), of posterity (Gen 17:6–8; 12:2a), and of a place in history (Gen 12:2b).

On that day the Lord made a covenant with Abram... (Gen 15:18).

Note, however, that God's intention is nevertheless to bless all His people in His creation (Gen 12:3; 18:18). Abraham, a changed man because of this new covenant relationship, a change symbolised by his change of name, has been chosen to be the channel of God's redemptive purposes for all of humanity, a channel which will continue through the line of Isaac and Jacob.

Abraham is obligated to keep the covenant which God has made with him (Gen 17:9), although only the sign of circumcision is spelled out as an actual demand upon the people of the covenant (Gen 17:10). Christians are used to interpreting circumcision in the light of Paul's teaching in Romans 2:25–29, where he stresses that true circumcision involves the willing and joyful surrender of the heart to God, not just the physical ritual associated with the foreskin. But this was appreciated by the people of Israel also, as we see in passages like Deuteronomy 10:12–16. Being in a covenant relationship with God brings its responsibilities, but, as always, in response to God's prior initiative.

It cannot be stressed enough that this covenant is the foundational one in the life of Israel. This is the call of Abraham, and thus the call of Isaac and Jacob too, and therefore the call of the Jewish people as a whole. What one usually finds is that Christians tend to think of Moses as the key person in Israel's life with God, whereas his significance, as we shall see, lies at the next stage of Israel's life. For this reason Paul turns to Abraham rather than to Moses when he is speaking about the inner nature of what it means to be Jewish (Rom 4).

3. *The covenant at Sinai.* Moses was the next Israelite leader chosen by God to mediate a covenant with Israel:

I am making a covenant with you... (Ex 34:10).

This covenant does not abrogate or overshadow the Abrahamic covenant, even though some Christians treat it in this manner. On the contrary, it assumes and functions within that covenant:

The Israelites groaned in their slavery...God heard their groaning and he remembered his covenant with Abraham, with Isaac and with Jacob.

Because he loved your forefathers and chose their descendants after them, he brought you out of Egypt by his Presence and his great strength... (Ex 2:23f; Deut 4:37).

Israel is already referred to as God's people (see, for example, Ex 4:22; Deut 8:5), her call remaining the one which came through Abraham. One might express it in this way: through Abraham God formed a people, and through Moses He created a national constitution for that people. There is, clearly, a great deal of stress on Israel's obligations concerning spiritual and ethical principles, as well as much emphasis on socio-economic and ritual laws, because the people of God must live in accordance with God's own holy nature (Lev 11:44). God is providing directions for the way His people must live, or, to put it another way, He is making His will known to Israel. As Paul says,

So then, the law is holy, and the commandment is holy,

righteous and good...the law is spiritual... (Rom 7:12, 14).

Note, however, that this distinct lifestyle is not simply an end in itself, but is intended to be a witness to all the nations (eg Deut 4:5–8), thus maintaining the overall perspective which God has made plain from the beginning. This is neatly summed up by the notion of Israel, within this covenant, as a 'priestly nation' (Ex 19:6), priests serving to mediate between God and people, so that Israel, a nation of priests, becomes the mediator between God and all the other nations. The prophets continued to remind Israel of this in every generation (eg Jer 4:1f).

The Sinai covenant, then, is a covenant of grace just like all the others. The mass of laws is not evidence of a legalistic relationship with God, but rather the necessary code of practice for people who now belong to God and want to know how to live lives which will please Him. (In much the same way non-Christians often assume that Christians are in some kind of bondage to God because they live in accordance with strict moral rules regarding sexual relations, business ethics, and the like. It is not perceived this way by Christians, whose relationship with God is based on love and joy, and who are grateful to know how to behave in the right ways to please God.)

4. *The covenant with David.* Israel had demanded a human king as well as the Lord because she had seen the advantages which this had brought to the nations which lived around her. The benefits would be two in nature: a) Protection from enemies (1 Sam 8:19–20). b) Spiritual and moral leadership (1 Sam 8:1–5).

God's reaction to this demand for a human king was, we are told, less than enthusiastic, since this seemed to reflect a turning away from complete trust in God Himself as Israel's King, able and willing to protect and guide His people (1 Sam 8:6–9; 10:17–19). However, a king was granted to Israel, and when Saul proved to be disobedient and unworthy of the trust put in him, God did not turn to the people to point out that this had been inevitable, and then refuse to grant them any further kings. From His grace and commitment to Israel, He not only continued to allow them a further series of kings, but actually initiated the election of a young shepherd to be king, making a covenant with David which promised that his descendants would always rule as the rightful kings in Jerusalem (see Psalm 89:1–4 where we are actually told that this relationship was in the nature of a covenant).

This covenant is the one which forms the basis of the Messianic dynasty from which Jesus himself is descended (see Is 11:1f; Ezek 34:22–24; Matt 1:17; 9:27–34; 12:22–24).

It should also be noted that, like the previous covenants, this one assumes the context of those which precede it. It exists for the benefit of Israel, not for the glorification of David's family. What is more, David himself, and all his descendants, are bound by the laws of Sinai, just like every other Israelite (see 2 Sam 7:14; 12:1–14).

5. *The New Covenant prophesied by Jeremiah.* This is the fifth of the major covenants set out for us in the Bible, and it is spoken of by the prophet in terms of a future rather than a present inauguration (Jer 31:31–

34). Jeremiah had probably experienced the great revival of spiritual and moral life under the leadership of king Josiah, after 'the Book of the Law' had been found in the temple (2 Kings 22—23). But he saw that the people's hearts were not sufficiently changed to make this a true and lasting reform of the nation's life (see Jer 2; 5; 11). So he sensed God's desire for a new covenant relationship altogether.

It is the promise of such a new relationship which we see in the prophecy of chapter 31, where the first thing highlighted is that this covenant will unite Israel and Judah, thus serving to reconcile and restore the kingdoms, divided since the death of Solomon. This means that the new covenant is not a matter for the Gentile nations of the world or the Church at the expense of the Jewish people. It concerns the very fabric of Israel's life.

The second thing to be noted is that nowhere is it said that there will be new laws in this new relationship, nor will there be any annulment of the laws or principles of previous covenants. It is the *people* who are at fault, according to Jeremiah, not the covenants of God. Ezekiel agrees that it is a new heart which is needed, not new laws from God (Ezek 36:25–27). One might well compare the perspective of Paul as we see it in Romans 7, where he spells out that in his conflict with God's Law, it is he himself who is at fault, not the Law, which is good, spiritual, and godly. Contrary to the opinion of many Christians, it is not the Law of God against which the Spirit of God is at war, but it is 'the flesh', our self-centred human nature against which the Spirit fights (see, for instance, Gal 5:16f; Rom 8:5–11).

The final aspect to be stressed here is this: even though the Church rightly interprets that this is the same new covenant which Jesus had in mind at the so-called Last Supper, when he inaugurated what we know as the sacrament of Holy Communion (Lk 22:20), and rightly interprets this as being a sacrament for all nations on the earth, the Church is quite wrong when it applies this prophecy to Christians at the expense of the Jewish people. I have stressed the point more than once that God's intention was always to bless all the peoples of the earth. We are all children of Adam, members together of the covenant with Noah, and inheritors of the promise to Abraham that all peoples would be blessed through him. This has all been wonderfully fulfilled in and through Jesus, but not in a way which has jettisoned the Jewish people as worthless material from the past.

The time has surely come for Christians to confess that they have constantly chosen to be greedy, preferring not to share any of God's blessing and promise with the Jewish people, and forgetting Paul's warning to us not to boast, but rather to remember that we are the wild branches who have been grafted in to the olive tree (Rom 11:12–24). The Church is always quick to refer to Hebrews 8:5–13, which speaks of the fading of the older covenant, but it must be kept in mind that the covenant referred to there is the one made at Sinai, not the constitutional one initiated with Abraham. The actual call of the Jewish people is still valid. God has no intention of leaving the Jewish people separated from the one olive tree. They are still within His loving purposes, still loved in the election-call of Abraham:

As far as the gospel is concerned, they are enemies on your account; but as far as election is concerned, they are loved on account of the patriarchs, for God's gifts and his call are irrevocable (Rom 11:28f).

And so we return to the question which haunts us, the question which will not allow us to settle for any answer which refuses to hold together in tension the reality of the biblical teaching that there is a God-given relationship between the two communities of Israel and the Church. What is it which remains special about the Jewish people and so makes the Church's relationship to the Jewish people unique? Let us see what help can be gained from an examination of those prophecies which speak of God turning Israel back to Himself in the end times. Can Christians agree here on the role and destiny of Israel?

# 4
# Biblical Prophecies And Modern Politics

This is a highly controversial subject, so perhaps it would be helpful if I set out in advance my own particular position vis-a-vis Christian relations to the modern State of Israel. I hope to show in the evidence and arguments of the chapter that it is our responsibility and privilege as Christians:

a) to support the sovereignty of the State of Israel, even though we must be free to disagree with one another on the proper borders, government policies, etc.

b) to pray and work for justice and peace between Jews and Arabs in Israel and the Middle East. The attitude towards, and treatment of, the Palestinian Arab people is of fundamental importance to God, as it should be to us as well.

c) to pray for Israel's national repentance, leading to faith in Jesus as her Messiah and Lord. Indeed we should not be ashamed to actually share the Gospel with Jewish people.

d) to be cautious in claiming that this or that biblical prophecy has been fulfilled in some contemporary incident: the State of Israel is only the beginning of what God is doing for and through the Jewish people.

These are four issues which I think no Christian can bypass in an attempt to deal with the subject of the biblical promises of Israel's restoration to the land of Israel, and how they relate to the present political situation in the Middle East.

## The Gift Of A Land

As we saw in the last chapter, when God called Abram into His service, one of the promises to him and his descendants was that they would receive the gift of a land which would be theirs in perpetuity (see Gen 12:7; 13:15; 15:18; 26:4; 28:13). At the end of the book of Genesis we see this promise threatened by Israel's captivity in Egypt, but God is faithful to His promises, rescuing Israel, and bringing her to the land of Canaan. It is made clear to Israel that the land belongs, by right, only to God Himself and that she rules over it by dint of God's gracious gift:

> The land must not be sold permanently, because the land is mine and you are but aliens and my tenants (Lev 25:23).

The Israelites are His stewards of the land, rather than people with their own claim to sovereignty. Nevertheless, Israel is the nation whom God has decreed will rule over the Promised Land. One might say, using legal terminology, that the land of Israel belongs to God de iure, and to Israel de facto. In other words, God alone has *rights* over the land, but Israel alone has His authority to rule over it as steward and manager. This is her *right* from God.

But it is not quite as simple as that, since God also makes it clear that He is prepared to punish Israel by exiling them from the land, should that become necessary, and Israel prove ever to be persistently disobedient to Him and dismissive of His rules for her behaviour (see Deut 28:15–68). This eventually happened, when God allowed Assyria to capture the northern kingdom of Israel (see 2 Kings 17:1–23), and then permitted the Babylonians to destroy and exile the southern kingdom of Judah (see 2 Kings 25:1–26). Once again we see the promises to Israel under extreme threat. Is this the end of the covenant relationship, the end of Israel's life as a distinct and sovereign nation? Has God abandoned His people in exile?

The answer to that last question is a very definite no, and it is important for us to note that the sending of Israel into exile is presented in the Bible as the withdrawal of God's blessing from Israel for the purpose of punishment and discipline, not as the removal of His love or commitment to Israel, nor of the pledge of His covenant promises. Indeed we see the later prophets regularly comforting Israel with the renewed promise of God's faithfulness and mercy, assuring her that God will one day restore them to sovereignty in their own land as a great nation (see Amos 9:15; Hos 11:11; Is 35:10; Jer 31:8; Ezek 36—39, as examples of this). There is no doubt in the minds of the prophets that God's intention is to restore Israel to a glorious future, worshipping God at last in the way which He deserves, led by a Davidic king, and bearing testimony to the sovereign grace and faithfulness of the Lord.

There was a partial fulfilment of that promise of restoration under the leadership of Ezra and Nehemiah (see Ezra 1:1–5; Neh 1:1—2:8), but it was a pale shadow of the glory promised by the prophets. It was also rather short-lived, since Israel fell under the oppressive yoke of the Greeks and then the Romans, suffering loss of sovereignty in the land of Israel yet again, apart from a brief recovery under the leadership of the famous Maccabees. The Romans finally dealt what seemed like the death blow to Jewish hopes when they destroyed Jerusalem in 70 AD and wiped out the last resistance at Masada in 73 AD. From that time until 1948 there was no Jewish State of any kind in the land of Israel, although there always was a significant community of Jewish people who actually lived in the country.

What about the vast majority of Jewish people though, those who lived in the Diaspora, scattered over the whole earth? For their part they never forgot the promises given by God of a glorious restoration of the people to the land, to renewed sovereignty in the land, and to a role in the final fulfilment of God's plan for creation. Synagogues were built to face Jerusalem; prayers were said daily in which God was asked to return in mercy to Zion, and also therefore to restore His people to Zion. Each year at Passover Jewish people expressed the hope that in the coming year they would be in Israel, celebrating the feast there. The people constantly longed for the freedom to return, to be saved from the life of misery and oppression which they were suffering among the nations of the world, especially, as we shall see in a later chapter, among the 'Christian' nations.

Therefore the Jewish people throughout the world never lost their desire to return to the land God had given them, even though they had no freedom to actually return there in any great numbers. The Jewish communities of the Diaspora were kept in political, social and economic degradation, making any thought of mass migration to 'Palestine', as it was then known, impossible. For a range of reasons, then, it was only in the second half of the 19th century that any real impetus was made in actually devising a plan for wholesale and organised movement back to the land of Israel by the Jewish people. It was the continued antisemitism of Europe which finally drove one very secularised Austrian Jewish journalist, Theodore Herzl, to initiate certain political moves. These eventually led, via massive pogroms in Eastern Europe, the famous Balfour Declaration of 1915, and the horrors of the Holocaust during the reign of Hitler in Germany, to the Declaration of the State of Israel in 1948.

## Prophecy Fulfilled?

The question which concerns us in this book is whether this very State of Israel could be the fulfilment of those biblical prophecies regarding the final restoration of Israel in the end days. Before we turn to the responses to that question which are given by Christians, it will be instructive to note the responses of the various Jewish religious groups. Christians might be forgiven for assuming that all Jewish people would be 100% behind the aims of Zionism to re-establish Jewish sovereignty and security in the land of their fathers, but this is not the case.

In the first place there were (and are) those Jews who insisted that the best future for Jews was to work towards a universal humanitarian culture which would transcend race, nation and religion. One way in which many Jewish people expressed this attitude was in their wholehearted acceptance of Marxist socialism. National liberation movements and religious causes were seen as a fruitless waste of human resources, since the only true struggle was for the freedom of the proletariat from the corruption of the ruling classes the world over. The terrible treatment of the Jewish people was a great shame, but its true solution lay in transcending Judaism and Jewishness, and in seeking a world reformation in the name of Adam, not Moses.

Then there were (and are) those Jewish people who insisted that they were part of a religious community, and that national aspirations were alien to right Jewish thinking, since Jewish people should simply wish to be good citizens of whichever country was theirs by birth. A classic statement to this effect was made in 1885 at Pittsburg, in the USA, when the American Reform Judaism conference produced the following as its fifth major point:

> We consider ourselves no longer a nation, but a religious community, and therefore expect neither a return to Palestine...nor the restoration of any of the laws concerning the Jewish state.

The third strand of opposition has tended to interest Christians most, since it comes from the ultra-Orthodox religious Jewish communities, and involves the issue of the Messiah. According to the theological framework of the Orthodox, the restoration of the Jewish people en masse to the land of Israel, as opposed to the decision of individual Jews to live there, is the prerogative of the Messiah alone. Therefore to initiate or accelerate the return of the Jewish nation was (and is) seen as irreligious presumption and an affront to the Messiah, betraying Israel's essentially covenant nature. The continued exile in the Diaspora is interpreted, in biblical perspective, as punishment for sin, so that only God can initiate and orchestrate Israel's restoration, consequent upon His forgiveness of her sin. Here is one quotation from one of Orthodox Judaism's most influential scholars, Rabbi Moses ben Maimon, which sets out the grounds for their opposition to the State of Israel very clearly:

> All the prophets spelled out the message of repentance; Israel will be redeemed only through repentance. The Torah had foretold that Israel was destined to repent at the end of their exile, and that they would forthwith be redeemed.

It is patently clear, they claim, that Israel is a secular State, governed in accordance with human definitions of power and political organisation, and not characterised by a turning to God in repentance and faith. It is thus not a candidate for the role of the promised Messianic kingdom of the last days.

It is necessary to add at this point that most

Orthodox Jewish people have in fact come to terms
with modern Zionism and the State of Israel. Only
the very Orthodox communities continue to refuse to
recognise the State. The Orthodox embrace of what
has been a political movement has involved the interpretation of modern history as God at work behind
the scenes, gradually preparing His people for a full
return in repentance and faith to Himself. God has
enabled the building of the present State in order to
have in place the clay from which He will mould the
true Messianic State in His own good time. Israel is
not, then, the fulfilment of biblical prophecy, but it is
the work of God, in preparation for His final intervention in history. This part of the work of God is
regularly referred to in Orthodox Jewish writings as
'the beginning of the time of redemption'.

What are Christians to make of all this? Many
seem to be saying that it is of no direct interest to
Christians, being purely a Jewish concern. Of course
Christians will form political opinions regarding the
rights of Israelis and Palestinians, etc, but that will
have no more significance than opinions about the
plight of North American Indians, or Armenians, for
example. However this is not the attitude of most
Christians, who sense that the issue of the fulfilment
of specific biblical prophecies is at stake here, and in
this chapter we must look at the issue of Christian
attitudes to the State of Israel. This is especially
important since it involves the basic matter of Christian attitudes towards the Jewish claim to the right to
continued national and religious sovereignty. There
are Christians who rejoice in this Jewish claim, wel-
coming and actively supporting it, but there are also

those Christians who deplore this attitude, condemning all Christian support for Israel, and indeed counter-claiming that the Jewish people are finished as in any sense special in God's eyes. Their support is for the Palestinian people, paying particular attention to the plight of the Christian communities among the Palestinians, and demanding that Christians realise that their first allegiance is to these brother and sister Christians, not to Jewish people.

When we turn to the New Testament we find that the matter is not cleared up for us in any unambiguous way. Jesus lived at a time when the Jewish people were subject to the power and rule of the Roman Empire. Moreover he was born into an age when there was a great deal of apocalyptic fervour, with much Jewish longing for a movement to drive the Romans out of the ancient homeland. One of Jesus' own disciples is referred to as 'Simon the Zealot', the zealots being a variety of political and military activists dedicated to driving out the Roman occupiers.

It was natural for people to wonder whether Jesus himself might be the one to lead such a popular revolt against the Romans. After all, the belief was that it would be the Messiah who would be successful in such a programme of restoration, and many people were beginning to entertain the possibility that Jesus might be this promised Messiah.

Jesus was aware of this, firmly resisting the attempts to politicise him and crown him as Israel's Messianic King, complete with earthly kingdom (Jn 18:36). Nonetheless, the hope for this kind of scenario never left the minds of those who chose to follow

Jesus, and even after the resurrection we see his disciples asking him when he would make his move to restore the political kingdom to Israel (Acts 1:6). Jesus' reply to their question is ambiguous:

> It is not for you to know the times or dates the Father has set by his own authority. But you will receive power...and you will be my witnesses... (Acts 1:7–8).

Are we to infer from this reply, as some Christians do, that Jesus is implying that there will be a future restoration of the kingdom, and that only the details concerning it are not to be given to his disciples? Surely, they reason, had Jesus wanted to teach us that there was never to be such a restoration, and that the only future for Israel was to lie in the totally spiritualised realm of internal personal relationship with God through Jesus himself, then he would have replied to the disciples' question unequivocally, telling them so. On the other hand, there are Christians who interpret this episode as Jesus saying that his disciples are out of order here, driving it home that the only important issue is that of bearing active witness to Jewish people and others the world over that Jesus is the Messiah, the Son of God, and the Saviour of the world. Both groups of Christians are trying to interpret an ambiguous word of Jesus.

Certainly the other writers of the New Testament give very little space to this subject. The issues of Jewish evangelism, and the evangelisation of the world, receive much attention, as do the issues involving the proper lifestyle and beliefs of the community of followers of Jesus, but the subject of the restoration of the Jewish people, whether believers in Jesus or not, to sovereignty in the land of Israel is hardly dealt with at all. Even here, however, we need to be aware of the different interpretation put upon this statistical fact by different Christian commentators. Most Christians have seen this as evidence that this matter is of no importance to New Testament faith, stating that this should not surprise us, since it is obvious that *all* of the promises of the Hebrew Bible have been 'spiritually' fulfilled in Christ. He is now the only 'holy place' as far as God Himself is concerned, the only physical area of any significance, all other physical symbols (eg the temple, the ark of the covenant, the land of Israel itself) serving merely as types and shadows to point towards Christ.

Here is a typical statement by a Christian who, working from this basic perspective, opposes Christian attempts to see any theological significance in the present State of Israel. Frank H. Epp wrote a book in 1970 in which he stated:

> Holiness is not...where Jesus once walked, but where he is walking today...Christians, especially Western Christians, should renounce their legal and spiritual claims to any holy place in Palestine [sic]...and proclaim to all the world that Christ and Christianity are not dependent on them for meaning and survival.

Other Christians, albeit a minority, have maintained that the silence of the New Testament on this matter of the land of Israel is to be interpreted rather as a passive confirmation of its central place in the theology of Israel, a place it would have kept even in the theological programme of those Jewish people, like Paul, who became believers in Jesus. Put baldly, their interpretation is that the restoration of Israel was so fundamental to Israel's theology that it is taken for granted by the New Testament authors, and for that reason alone is not expounded along with the teaching on justification by faith, atonement through the death of Jesus, etc.

Someone who has been very influential in spreading this type of interpretation is Lance Lambert, who wrote in 1980 regarding Jesus' reply to his disciples in Acts 1:6–8:

> Jesus...did not deny that at some point in time Jewish sovereignty would be restored. In fact, the very way in which he answered their question implies that it would be restored.

Thus we see the two approaches to this problem set out before us. There can be no doubt that this has been one of the major issues in Jewish-Christian relations in recent generations, and that it continues to hold a prominent place in the debate. The various millenarian schemes of the first centuries of the Christian era, in which Christians developed their understanding of the second coming of Jesus and his 1,000 year reign from Jerusalem, make no clear reference to any serious debate about the political restoration of the Jewish people. Moreover, it is doubted whether any such Christian idea would have commanded any real support in the context of the movement towards theological and socio-political self-definition by the Jewish and Christian communities. As we know, these self-definitions became mutually exclusive. However, from the early Middle Ages there developed some measure of support for a vision of such a restoration of the Jewish people, but it was always a minority view.

With the Reformation, however, in the 16th century, the Protestant churches developed a new focus on messianism and millenarianism, leading to a consequent reappraisal of the place of the Jewish people in God's purposes. Church leaders and thinkers began to teach that God had indeed promised in the Bible that He would restore the Jewish people to sovereignty in 'the Holy Land' as part of His plan for the Messianic kingdom. This stream of thought began to flow more strongly, especially in Holland and England, thereafter moving across the ocean to North America. Known by historians as the 'Restoration Movement' (not to be confused with the contemporary movement of the same name), it was largely inspired by the teaching of the New Testament about Jesus' second coming, and his millenial rule from restored Jerusalem. As this gathered momentum through the 18th and into the 19th century, various Christian groups and individuals came to support the position that God did indeed intend to bring back the Jewish people to the land He had promised to Abraham. This restoration, which would involve wholesale returning to God by the Jewish people, centred on the recognition of Jesus as their Messiah, would lead inexorably to the return of Jesus himself to his rightful throne in Jerusalem.

Though this never became the official position of the mainline churches, the list of those who did adopt it, in one form or another, is very impressive. Mention can be made here (in chronological order) of a few famous individuals, like Oliver Cromwell, John

Milton, Sir Isaac Newton, John Adams (the second President of the United States of America), Lord Byron, Lord Shaftesbury, Benjamin Disraeli, Robert Browning and Sir Winston Churchill. It has also become part of the official teaching of groups as diverse as the Plymouth Brethren, the Christadelphians and the Mormons. Recent history has shown that this position has also become central to the various Dispensationalist systems held by many evangelical Christians throughout the world.

What is it, then, which prevents all the churches from adopting this same position? Is it simply a refusal to allow any continuing validity for the Jewish people in the light of a theology which declares that only the Church is heir to the promises of the Hebrew Bible? If the Jewish people are no longer religiously significant, then there can be no religious significance for the State of Israel either. This is indeed a commonly raised objection to Christian support for the restoration of the State of Israel, but in fact it is only one of several lines of argument given by different Christian groups as to why there is to be no restoration of Israel. Apart from this rejectionist position, which sees no future for the Jewish people at all in God's special plans for the world (a position we shall examine carefully in the next chapter), what other objections are there?

Firstly, there are those Christians who believe that the State of Israel cannot be the fulfilment of any prophecy since there has been no national repentance on behalf of the Jewish people, this being an equal aspect of those same prophetic passages in the

Hebrew Bible which speak of a national restoration. Here is a typical example:

> when you and your children return to the Lord your God and obey him with all your heart and with all your soul according to everything I command you today, then the Lord your God will restore your fortunes and have compassion on you and gather you again from all the nations where he scattered you (Deut 30:2–3; see also, eg Ezek 36:24–26, 33; 1 Kings 8:47–50; Jer 18:5–10).

The fact that the modern State of Israel is not made up of people who have returned to the Lord in repentance and faith is taken as sufficient evidence that the biblical prophecies have not been fulfilled since 1948.

Then there are those who believe that Jesus' second coming must surely precede any kind of national reconstitution of the Jewish people, so that no matter how impressive the contemporary phenomenon of the establishment of the State of Israel may be, and even though we will want to impress upon the world our conviction that God is behind all the forces of history, moving the nations according to His own purposes, we shall nevertheless be unable to speak of the present State of Israel as the actual fulfilment of prophecy.

Many Christians hold that to the extent that there ever was a physical and political restoration intended by the prophets in the Hebrew Bible, passages like Jeremiah 29:10 and Daniel 9:2 refer to the return from exile in Babylon under Ezra and Nehemiah. In other words, all the references to renewed sovereignty were relevant only to the situation long before the coming of Jesus. Since the time of Jesus, they argue, the only restoration intended by God is directed to our spiritual rapprochement with God through faith in Jesus.

There are Christians from another theological camp altogether, whose dominant commitment is to an ecumenical universalism which has no room for any Jewish particularity or special claim to significance. Indeed their understanding is that God is only interested in Everyman, not in any particular people at all. Very often this criticism is coupled with one which is based on what are presented as moral priorities: general humanitarian attitudes, focused as often as not on the plight of the Palestinians, must outweigh any specific theological arguments for the superiority of one religious people-group over any other. It is regarded as self-evident that no reading of the prophets can be right if it infringes on the basic human rights of other peoples.

A word should be also said here about the position of the Roman Catholic Church. In 1904 Theodore Herzl, the founder of modern political Zionism, obtained an interview with Pope Pius X, who responded to Herzl's request for support of the Zionist movement with these famous words:

> We are unable to favour this movement...The Jews have not recognised our Lord, therefore we cannot recognise the Jewish people.

When the State of Israel was actually declared in 1948 a spokesman at the Vatican said:

> Modern Zionism is not the authentic heir of biblical

Israel, but constitutes a lay-state...This is why the Holy Land and its sacred places belong to Christianity, the veritable Israel.

Although the thinking of the Roman Catholic Church vis-a-vis the Jewish people has undergone vast changes since the seminal work of Vatican Two in the 1960s, and influential Roman Catholic theologians are encouraging the Vatican to recognise the State of Israel, it has still not done so. It is partly as a result of the traditional supersessionist theology of the church, and partly due to the Vatican's expressed concern for the safety and well-being of Arab Christians in the Middle East who might be exposed to persecution if political support were given to Israel.

What we need to do is to find a mediating way between rejection of Israel and the full-blooded 'Christian Zionism', so called, of those who see Israel as the key to all of God's work in the world today. Modern political Zionism is secular, it is not centred on the desire to seek the will of God. A *biblical* Zionism, which is surely the desire of every Christian, will be fundamentally about God and His purposes. Thus Zionism, when seen in a proper Christian perspective, will be understood as a branch of theology, not of politics. This does not mean that there will be no political implications or applications, but support for any given decision or action in Israel will have to be judged in accordance with the full range of biblical principles, and not in some unconditional manner. In the same way there should be no such thing as unconditional support for every decision or action taken by the churches or any 'Christian country'.

92 / *The Covenant With The Jews*

The continued life and vitality of the Jewish people is one of the great signs of the faithfulness and power of God. God is preserving His chosen people. But in our awe at the graciousness of God, let us not forget that very particular group of Jewish people who are invariably left out of the writings of Zionists, both Jewish and Christian—namely the Jewish people who have come to faith in Jesus as Israel's true Messiah. Jesus' priority was to Jewish people, not non-Jews (see Matt 10:5–6; 15:21–28), and all the New Testament writers were quite convinced that the Gospel was intended for Jewish people. It took a great deal of persuasion for the first generation of believers to accept that the Gospel was meant for non-Jews at all (see Acts 10:1—11:18). Paul himself, though set apart by God to be an apostle to non-Jews, nevertheless taught that the Gospel was first of all a gift to the Jewish people, agonising over the fact that the majority of his people rejected Jesus as their promised Messiah (see Rom 1:16; 9:1–3).

Let me state again what I have set out earlier as a fundamental perspective of the Bible: if the Gospel has nothing to say to Jewish people, then it has nothing to say to anyone. If Jesus is not Israel's Messiah then he is no-one's Messiah, no-one's Christ. Christians cannot leave this truth out of the equation when we consider the relationship of the restoration of the Jewish people to sovereignty in the land of Israel, to that of the purposes of God for Israel and the world. The survival of the Jewish people *is* a great sign to all of us of God's control of history, and the establishment of the State of Israel *is* a great sign that God is bringing His people back for their appointment with destiny. But the *greatest* sign of God's faithfulness and commitment to His covenant purposes is the (growing) number of Jewish believers in Jesus. In chapter six we shall devote all of our attention to these brothers and sisters.

Perhaps, then, it would be acceptable to conclude this presentation of the issues surrounding the question of the relationship of the State of Israel to God's biblical prophecies concerning the Jewish people, with the four principles with which I opened the chapter: it is our responsibility and privilege as Christians

a) to support the sovereignty of the State of Israel, even if we must be free to disagree with one another on the proper borders, government policies, etc.

b) to pray and work for justice and peace between Jews and Arabs in Israel and the Middle East. The attitude towards, and treatment of, the Palestinian Arab people is of fundamental importance to God, as it should be to us as well.

c) to pray for Israel's national repentance, leading to faith in Jesus as her Messiah and Lord. Indeed we should not be ashamed to actually share the Gospel with Jewish people.

d) to be cautious in claiming that this or that biblical prophecy has been fulfilled in some contemporary incident: the State of Israel is only the beginning of what God is doing for and through the Jewish people.

I realise that such an acceptance of responsibility vis-a-vis the State of Israel will not be at all easy to achieve, because of the Church's legacy of rejection of all Jewish claims to on-going relationship with God. Tragically, not only has the Church traditionally championed this theology which excludes the Jewish people from any positive role in God's plans, but this theological rejection has spilled over into an attitude of contempt for Jewish people themselves. We must look at this situation before we go any further.

# 5
# Are Any Of Your Best Friends Jewish?

Anyone who knows anything about the history of antisemitism will recognise here one of the most famous by-lines used by people who are antisemitic. You still hear people make scathing attacks on the Jewish community, condemn the Jewish people in stereotypically racist or prejudiced terms, but then seek to cover themselves from any criticism by adding the words, 'Of course not all Jews are like that—some of my best friends are Jewish!' Jewish people are sensitive to these types of remarks, aimed at camouflaging the real attitude of the speaker. Sadly, we must admit that this is not a sign of paranoia among Jewish people, but based on centuries of both verbal and physical abuse by the peoples among whom they have lived. People in the West, especially Christians, do not like to admit this fact, hence the attempt to cover their own prejudices by mentioning exceptions to the rule, namely particular friends or colleagues.

Most tragic of all, perhaps, is the fact that it is in the so-called Christian countries that much of the worst of this contempt for, and oppression of, the Jewish people has happened. How can it be that those who follow Jesus, the Prince of Peace, the man who himself was a Jewish person, have treated the Jewish people so abominably? Stories can be told of how Christians have ridden rough-shod over other peoples and cultures, and of how churches have become involved in the nastier side of power politics. But nothing compares to the persistent and consistent animosity directed towards Jewish people. Because this is so, Christian antisemitism is probably the single most important factor in Jewish-Christian relations today.

There are, in fact, three terms which are found commonly in use today: antisemitism, anti-Judaism and anti-Zionism. Even though most writers still spell the first term as anti-semitism, this is really an unfortunate custom, since there is no such thing as 'semitism' which one can be against. Jewish people are only one of the family of Semitic peoples (the other major group being the Arab peoples). The term 'antisemitism' was coined last century in Germany to specifically describe the attitude of hatred towards Jews, and active oppression of Jews. Antisemitism is expressed in all manner of contexts: irrational feelings of superiority to Jewish people, caricaturing of physical features, economic boycotting of Jewish businesses, social ostracism of Jewish people, organised destruction of Jewish homes and property and murder of Jewish people. Christians are not innocent in this regard.

Anti-Judaism, on the other hand, describes the attitude which opposes 'Judaism' as an authentic religious tradition, either being satisfied with denigrating it vis-a-vis another religious tradition (eg Christianity), or wishing to go further by writing it off altogether. Common expressions of this from Christians are often in the form of (mistakenly) condemning Judaism as a religion of dry legalism, or as a religion based on the system of scoring points with God through human effort at righteousness. This is then contrasted with the picture of Christianity as a faith based on God's gracious love to humanity, a faith which creates a community of freedom and sacrificial love. Such an attitude of anti-Judaism refuses to look at the realities of Jewish life and teaching, and rejects the invitation of Jesus to love our neighbour as ourselves, in this case by letting Jewish people define their own faith from within. Ignorance was never a virtue.

The third term, anti-Zionism, is used by those who take a stance against the aims and methods of the Zionist political philosophy regarding the State of Israel. People might also be, for example, anti the Scottish Nationalist Party and its presuppositions and goals, without in any way being antagonistic to the Scottish people. In fact many Scottish people themselves campaign against the SNP. In the same way, some Jewish people, including some who actually live in the State of Israel, and for various reasons, take a stance against modern Zionism. Others insist on a quite new approach to, and definition of Zionism, before they could identify themselves as Zionist Jewish people.

One of the great issues facing us is whether it is possible to be anti-Judaic or anti-Zionist without also being antisemitic. Many people will immediately respond in the affirmative. You can be a strong opponent of current British foreign policy, or of the moral climate in contemporary British society, without being at all anti-British, so why not the same with respect to Jewish political or religious beliefs? It is important to point out that antisemitism is not necessarily the root which is supporting criticisms of Jewish religious or political ideologies. One is disconcerted to come across Jewish people accusing other Jewish people of being 'antisemitic' in a perverted self-hate sort of way, simply because they have convictions which are critical of the Jewish mainstream of thought.

This point seems fair enough, but we must also remember that claims to being anti-Judaic or anti-Zionist are very often simply the socially acceptable way for non-Jews to express hostility to the Jewish people per se. People cover up their prejudice by disguising it as political or theological critique, and it is indisputable that antisemitism does lie at the heart of much anti-Judaism and anti-Zionism in the world and in the Church.

Christians did not invent antisemitism, nor were they the first to use the Jewish people as convenient scapegoats for the ills of society, but they did inject a new source of hostility, and its roots lie in the area of religious self-identity. Christians were (and are) terribly frustrated at the fact that most Jewish people rejected (and continue to reject) the Messiahship of Jesus. After the destruction of the temple by the

Romans in AD 70, which meant that sacrifices were no longer possible, the Jewish people regrouped under what we now know as Rabbinic Judaism, developed from the religious traditions of the pharisees. Relatively few Jewish people came to believe that Jesus was in fact the once-and-for-all sacrifice for the sins of the world, God's promised Messiah.

Here lies what was seen as the great dilemma: of *all* people, it is precisely the Jewish people who *should* believe in Jesus. He himself was Jewish, both ethnically and religiously; the God he called 'Abba' was the same God of the patriarchs; his Bible was the Hebrew Scriptures; who else but the Jews would know what a 'Messiah' was, let alone follow him as the decisive revelation of God? Why should other people and peoples follow Jesus if his own people, the ones who were waiting for the Messiah to come, said he was not the promised Messiah? Why should other peoples accept the Church as the people of God, when the Jewish people were continuing to make that claim for themselves, attracting their own 'converts' along the way? In other words, what was developing into what we now call Judaism, and what became the dominant religious interpretation of the Jewish people, was seen as a great embarrassment and threat to the Gospel and to the Church.

To the Church's shame, however, this theological frustration was allowed, and indeed encouraged in some quarters, to translate into attitudes of hatred towards Jewish people. There was plenty of argumentation at the theological level to be found in sermons and books, but it rarely escaped degeneration into attacks on the actual integrity of the Jewish people. It was commonly said that the only possible explanation for their refusal to acknowledge Jesus as Israel's Messiah was that God Himself had placed some terrible curse on the Jewish people for crucifying Jesus. The fact that it was the Romans who actually executed Jesus, and that only some of the Jewish leadership connived in the whole process, did not stand in the way of the accusation that 'the Jews' were 'Christ killers', or even 'God killers'.

History has shown us that it is a very short step from having such a contemptuous view of people to coming to see them as somehow less than human, and perhaps not human at all. Many preachers and scholars went this far, and actually 'demonised' the Jewish people, saying that they were demons in human guise. Once this point has been reached, it can prove all too easy to justify the maltreatment and persecution of people, because they are no longer seen as real human beings to be treated in humane ways. Many others have suffered in the same way in various times and cultures of course—travelling people, indigenous peoples, slaves, women, etc.

The real trouble for Jewish people began in the 4th century, when the Roman emperor, Constantine, converted to Christianity, consequently decreeing that this was now to be the sole official religion of the empire. The Church became married to the State, and it was not long before she began to translate her anti-Judaism (wed indissolubly by this time to anti-semitism) into political oppression of the Jewish communities throughout the empire. For centuries thereafter the trend continued: synagogues were often officially referred to by a word meaning a brothel; 'Jews' were forbidden to hold high civic office; 'Jews' were forbidden from testifying against Christians in court; 'Jews' had to wear distinct, and demeaning, articles of clothing so that Christians could either avoid them or pick on them, depending on what they wanted to do; 'Jews' were forbidden to own land or be farmers; 'Jews' could not learn or practice a trade or profession without joining the relevant guild, all of which were constitutionally Christian; etc, etc.

The final result was that Jewish people were forced into the only profession which Christians were not able to practise themselves, namely that of moneylending. The problem was that according to the Bible it is forbidden to take interest from fellow believers, thus closing that profession to Christians, and yet Christians often found themselves in the situation of needing to borrow money for various transactions. The solution which was found was that Jewish people were forced into moneylending by the Christian society around them.

This fact has resulted in two developments which have both been severely detrimental to the Jewish people: a) It exacerbated antisemitism by encouraging people to think of 'Jews' as people who persecute poor Christians by demanding interest from them on top of the repayment of financial loans, loans which themselves had only been necessary in the first place because the Christians were already in need. b) It led to the most common antisemitic stereotype and slur of them all, namely that Jews are interested only in money, and control all the money markets.

Another dimension of Christian hatred of Jewish people was to be revealed in the Middle Ages, during the times of the Crusades, when the Christian rulers and armies of Europe were marching to the Holy Land to liberate it from the Muslims. A large percentage of the great crowds of men who joined the crusader forces was more intent on making fortunes, venting their bitter frustrations on alien enemies, or just escaping from the drudge of their everyday lives, than in waging a pure spiritual war against the infidel Muslims. Some of the popular Christian leaders incited these men to acts of aggression against Jewish communities en route to Palestine by asking, 'Why go all that way to kill the enemies of Christ when we have his actual killers here among us?' And so the crusaders destroyed Jewish settlements and massacred Jewish men, women and children wherever they found them on their route to the Holy Land. Thereafter, the Jewish people experienced many such 'pogroms', as they came to be called, especially in what we now call Eastern Europe. Indeed the very word pogrom is a Russian term for a destructive attack on one community by another.

There is no space to give details about the hideously false accusation that Jews kidnap Christian boys every year at Passover, so that they may drain them of their blood. Christians taught that unleavened bread needed this blood in order to be made to the correct recipe. Nor can we give details of the wholesale expulsions of Jewish people from England and other European countries once they had been bled dry through economic exploitation by the ruling Christian classes. Nor can we set out the story of the infamous Spanish Inquisition, when the most dreadful and dehumanising tortures were inflicted upon Jewish people. Is it any real wonder that Jewish people do not trust Christians? Can it come as a surprise to learn that Jewish people do not want anything to do with the Church?

Christians were not even satisfied with negative strictures on the Jews, however. 'Positive' means were also developed for leading Jews to faith in Christ. Jews were made to attend church services in some places, having to contribute to the collection plate for the privilege of hearing their faith and character assassinated, before being exhorted to convert to Christianity. Sometimes there were friars who were sent into Jewish synagogues to preach to the Jews on the Sabbath, and, needless to say, attendance was compulsory. There were also some famous public 'Disputations' arranged throughout the Middle Ages, in which rabbis were 'invited' to formally debate the merits of Judaism and Christianity with prominent Church theologians. Sometimes these theologians themselves were Jews who had 'converted' to Christianity. The Jewish community came to hate and fear these occasions, because they were put into a no-win situation: should the Christian scholar 'win' the Disputation, then immense pressure would be brought to bear on the Jewish community to convert, with subsequent reprisals should they decline the invitation. On the other hand, should the Jewish representative dare to 'win', which really meant should he do at all well, then the Jewish community would face the offended pride and rage of the Christian populace. Either way, trouble was bound to follow.

Another favourite method of community evangelisation was that of forced baptism. Whole Jewish communities were given the choice of baptism or confiscation of property, baptism or expulsion, even baptism or death. Gregory the Great, however, was more inclined to the carrot than the stick, offering to reduce the rent of any Jew who acceded to baptism! It soon became the official teaching of the Church that once a Jew was baptised, then he/she was irretrievably baptised and a member of the Church, whatever the circumstances which had led to the 'conversion' and baptism. Even the kidnapping and forced baptism of Jewish children was not uncommon, with many children thereby being lost to their families and brought up by the Church in special institutions.

There were Christians who opposed all of this, of course, kings and popes among them, but they do not represent the dominant voice of the Church throughout this dark period.

Even when we come to the age after the Reformation, the Renaissance, and the Enlightenment, the story continues, albeit in different ways. Martin Luther seemed to begin his life as a friend of the Jewish people, himself condemning the treatment that Jews had suffered at the hands of Christians, but by the end of his life he was spouting antisemitic statements which could rival those of anyone else. Even though many of Luther's remarks have been taken out of context by later commentators, the fact remains that much of what he said was terribly intolerant, offensive, and conducive to attitudes of contempt and violence against the Jewish people.

Here are one or two examples of Luther's later writings on the Jewish people by way of illustration. It is particularly important for Protestants to see this, since some seem to imagine that such attitudes were confined to leaders of the Roman Catholic Church. What could be worse than these sayings of Luther?

> The Jews, being foreigners, should possess nothing, and what they do possess should be ours...Know, O adored Christ, and make no mistake, that aside from the Devil, you have no enemy more venemous, more desperate, more bitter, than a true Jew who truly seeks to be a Jew...their synagogues should be set on fire...and this ought to be done for the honour of God and of Christianity...their homes should likewise be broken down and destroyed...In short, they are children of the Devil...

This kind of teaching permeated the whole of European society, right into our own time in fact. Here are some instances of this very fact. At the end of the last century, France, seen by many as the epitome of civilised Christian culture in Europe, was shaken by the antisemitism which was exposed in the infamous Dreyfus Case, in which a Jewish soldier was court-martialled, unjustly, on the charge of being a spy for another government. The whole corrupt procedure of the court case was only possible because Captain Dreyfus was Jewish. Had he not been Jewish, things would have been done quite differently.

In a totally different cultural milieu, terrible pogroms continued to be waged upon Jewish communities in Eastern Europe, echoing to the cry of 'Christ killers!' Whole villages and communities were massacred by soldiers and peasants carrying crosses as well as weapons of death in their hands.

Right up until very modern times, it was impossible for a Jewish person to be accepted in Christian society, and certainly to become successful in the arts, the sciences, education, or the government, unless he/she became a baptised convert into the Church. Countless Jewish people decided to take the cynical route to success and security by agreeing to baptism and official conversion to Christianity. A typical example would be that of Heinrich Heine (1797-1856), one of Germany's outstanding poets. He was named Hayyim by his parents, but took his Christian name, Heinrich, upon his baptism into the Lutheran church in 1825. He was determined to pursue a university career which would open the doors for a profession in civil service or literary academia. To do this he had to 'become a Christian', and in his famous comment at the time he spoke of his baptismal certificate as his 'admission ticket to European culture'.

Simple statistics about 'Jewish Christians' are therefore no real indication of faith commitment, since very many of these Jewish people were just playing a political game. Of course there were also many genuine commitments to Jesus, but it is difficult now to try to determine the relative percentages, even though it is generally conceded today that the number of authentic professions of faith was far higher than earlier generations tended to allow. Because of this phenomenon of socially and politically motivated conversions, the Jewish community has convinced itself that such motives are the *only* ones which could lie behind any Jewish person's voluntary conversion and baptism. The assumption is always that the person converted, for example, for the sake of money, or a better job, or better marriage prospects.

As if this were not enough, it is all compounded by the fact that right up until today the basic message of the Church to Jewish people who 'become Christians' has been that they must renounce their Jewishness. They are no longer Jews, and are no longer to regard themselves as Jews. They are now to regard themselves purely as Christians, which is itself interpreted to mean that they are now Gentiles. As such they must adopt all of the customs, traditions, and ways of thinking of the dominant Gentile-Christian culture. They must eat pork to prove their freedom from the legalism of Judaism; they must not celebrate Passover or any other 'Jewish' feast; they must not circumcise their sons. Of course all of this reinforces the image of the Gospel as being anti-Jewish! To make matters even worse, history is sadly full of examples of Jewish people who 'converted to Christianity' and then turned viciously on their former communities in order to prove their complete shift of loyalty from the Synagogue to the Church. Christians today would be reluctant to consider these Jewish converts as true Christians, and would suspect that they converted in a situation of coercion, but nonetheless the memory of these incidents is kept fresh within the Jewish community.

Is it any wonder that Jewish people today want nothing to do with the Church or with Christians; that they see those Jewish people who do become believers in Jesus as traitors, betraying the memory of the countless Jewish martyrs who died at the hands of Christians; that they assume that any Christians who speak of evangelism among Jews are likely to be unscrupulous exploiters of vulnerable Jewish people?

Finally, our attention must be brought to bear on the terrible fact of the Holocaust. It is seen by the Jewish people as the culmination of all of the centuries of antisemitism, particularly Christian antisemitism. Right in the heart of Christian Europe unfolded the plot to rid the world at last of the 'problem' of the Jews. Hitler and his advisors, baptised people in full communion with the Church, were able to draw upon Medieval Catholic as well as Lutheran sayings and practices to justify their own particular brand of demonisation of the Jews. Christian governments all over the world turned a blind eye to what was happening. They refused to investigate the rumours, as they would have done had they been about Christians who were being systematically exterminated for their faith. They refused to open their borders to help absorb the many thousands of Jews who were desperately trying to escape. The story of Christians who *did* fight against this treatment of Jews is important and very moving, but again it is the account of a depressingly small minority. The immediate trauma of the Holocaust will remain with us for some time to come, and Christians should be under no illusion that it will ever be forgotten. Indeed, in the light of all that has been said in this chapter, they should be insisting that it not be forgotten!

Christians need to be made aware of their appalling record vis-a-vis the Jewish people, in order to prevent any attitude of easy triumphalism, or any tendency to feel superior as the 'religion of love' over against the Jewish religion of barren law. Public repentance on behalf of the Church is called for, and we should be pleased to see that this is happening in certain parts of, and at certain levels of, the churches today.

Going beyond this though, there are Christian voices today which are insisting that Christians have lost the moral right to try to share the Gospel with Jewish people. Christians are disqualified, they say, by reason of their spiritual and moral bankruptcy. Our first response as evangelicals to this claim should be to admit its force. Certainly no Christian should be thinking of witnessing to Jewish people without feeling shame at what has been done in the name of Jesus, and without realising the pain which will be caused by the sharing of the Gospel. Such great sensitivity is required from us!

Secondly, we must look at the option chosen by a large sector of the evangelical Protestant world, namely to declare that all of this persecution of the Jewish people was done by those who may have claimed to be Christians, but who in fact were not. This strategy seeks to distance 'true Christians' from the institutional churches (particularly Roman Catholic and Russian Orthodox), thus protecting both Jesus himself, and these contemporary Christians, from any responsibility or blame. It is perhaps felt most sharply in debates about the Holocaust, where young Christians insist on pointing out that they were born in a later generation, and so cannot be imputed with any blame for what was done during the war years. While it would certainly be wrong to try to make any such individual Christians feel personal guilt for what happened in the past, it is nonetheless also true that as long as they claim to be part of the universal Church, then they will have to share in the shame of the Church. Any great insistence on distancing oneself from the Church will therefore bring the risk of being seen simply as trying to run away from community responsibility and commitment. Sharing in the public repentance of the Church is a necessary aspect of Christian-Jewish relations today, even for young evangelicals.

It must also be said that there is more than one way to respond to the awful and distorted image of Jesus that the Church has given to Jewish people down the generations. One way is certainly to call a moratorium on presenting any image of Jesus at all, by withdrawing from all active witness, as many are now advocating. The other way is humbly to offer a corrected and authentic presentation of Jesus, the Jewish Messiah. But is this still really possible? Can the Church still speak out the name of Jesus with any integrity to the Jewish community? We turn to this issue in our next chapter.

# 6
# 'First For The Jew, Then For The Gentile'!

These words were written by Paul at the beginning of his letter to the church in Rome, stressing that the Gospel is the power of God at work, effecting salvation for all who believe. Included within his vision of 'all who believe' are the Jewish people, he himself being a Jewish believer. Not only that, but the Gospel has a spiritual priority for the Jewish people, and should be seen to be the power of God first for the Jew, and then for the Gentile. This is not to say that non-Jews are mere second-class citizens, but that the Good News originated within the specific salvation-history of the Jewish people. There is no point in expecting the Gospel to have relevance for others if it has none for the original recipients of the message. We have just been looking at the terrible history of Christian antisemitism, and how some Christians, painfully aware of this history, are therefore directing the Church to abandon any attempts to reach Jewish people with the Gospel. Is it possible to be sensitive to the reasoning behind this position and yet to maintain an insistence that there is still a place for appropriate forms of Jewish evangelism?

There are, in fact, Christians who seem to turn the antisemitism debate on its head, claiming that if the Gospel is the most central and wonderful part of your life, and you believe that this could and should also be the case for *all* people, then to deny the Gospel to Jewish people would itself constitute a form of anti-semitism. In 1989, for example, a group of inter-nationally acclaimed evangelical scholars issued what has come to be known as 'The Willowbank Declaration on the Christian Gospel and the Jewish People', part of which reads as follows:

> failure to preach the Gospel to the Jewish people would be a form of anti-Semitism.

What is being expressed here is the conviction that there is no greater joy in life, and indeed no other way to experience God's salvation, than through relationship with Jesus. Many Christians who believe that this also holds true for Jewish people go much further, and are convinced by their reading of passages like Romans 1:16, quoted above, that in fact Jewish evangelism is the key to the *whole* evangelistic programme of the Church. This should be the heart of the Church's whole missionary task and strategy. Here are the words of Moishe Rosen, himself a Jew-ish Believer in Jesus, and who is the Director of an organisation dedicated to Jewish evangelism:

> God's formula (in mission) is to bring the Gospel to

the Jews first...A low view of Jewish evangelism leads to an overall defective missiology.

We are seeing here the reiteration of the basic point made in previous chapters, namely that if the Gospel is not relevant to Jewish people then it cannot be relevant to anyone else. Hence the insistence on placing Jewish evangelism at the heart of the whole endeavour. Of course there are other Christians who agree that Jewish people need to hear the Gospel, just as much as all other peoples, and yet who stop short of stating that priority must be given to them. These Christians will simply want to make sure that Jewish evangelism is there on the Church's agenda along with the evangelisation of other peoples. Billy Graham, for instance, has gone on record as saying that he believes that Jewish people need to know Jesus as their Saviour just as much as non-Jews, but he adds:

> In my evangelical efforts I have never been called to single out Jews as Jews.

The difficulty for most evangelicals today, however, is that there seems to be a rising number of voices condemning any positive attitude to Jewish evangelism *in principle*. On the one hand there are those who do not come from an evangelical perspective, and who advocate an understanding of Judaism which sees it as perfectly sufficient, without Jesus, for the salvation of the Jewish people. Jewish people are already understood to be in an existing covenant relationship with God, and therefore have no need for the relationship made possible for non-Jews by the death of Jesus:

> It would be a total denial of our own Way if we even pretended to show it to Jews, for they already have their own way of being in the Way. (Paul van Buren)

But on the other hand there are evangelicals whose dispensational programmes rule out the possibility of any widespread Jewish turning to faith in Jesus until he himself returns to earth. That will be the time when the Jewish people will recognise Jesus for who he really is. In the meantime, in this present dispensation, the task of Christians is to stand with the Jewish people, and to comfort the State of Israel politically and economically, as an expression of repentance for, and as an inadequate act of restitution for, the atrocities committed against the Jewish people by past Christian generations. In a recent magazine published by the International Christian Embassy in Jerusalem, for example, we find the leadership of that organisation proudly quoting from an Israeli politician who said of them that, 'They are the finest example of Christian Zionism.' Their only concept of mission is 'to convert the Jews to Judaism and to gather Jews—not in Christianity, but in planes to Israel.'

What are Christians to believe? The whole issue is made the more urgent today by the fact that some churches, led in part by the Church of England, have declared the 1990s to be a 'Decade of Evangelism'. Will this mean a renewed effort to share the Gospel with people of different faiths, including the Jewish people? Of particular interest has been the role of the

Archbishop of Canterbury, the senior bishop in the Church of England, and what is more, a man who has given his personal blessing to the decade of evangelism. The Archbishop was in a delicate position from the moment of his enthronement, for the reason that he inherited with his office the roles of being both the Patron of CMJ and one of the Presidents of CCJ. The significance of this is that CMJ (The Church's Ministry among the Jews) is the Anglican Church's own agency of Jewish evangelism, whereas CCJ (The Council of Christians and Jews) is an organisation dedicated to dialogue *at the expense of evangelism.* How could the Archbishop fulfil his obligations to both organisations at the same time?

As is well known by now, the Archbishop himself decided that he could not maintain this kind of official link with both of these organisations, both of which claimed to reflect the authentic voice of the Scriptures and the Church. Dr Carey made it clear that he saw himself in a position of authority to help protect the rights of faith communities in Britain other than the Christian ones. He also intimated that many of the current tactics of Jewish evangelism were unacceptable to his sense of ethical propriety, although he conceded that no such tactics were employed by CMJ. After many months of waiting, he declined the office of Patron of CMJ, while re-emphasising his commitment to the philosophy and practice of CCJ. The clear signal to the Church (and the Synagogue) was that it is impossible to keep a foot in both camps.

This is in fact the central question facing Christians today. We are told both by Jewish people and by some Christians that it is impossible to be involved in both dialogue and evangelism. The message is that you cannot be a real receiver and listener if you are also convinced that what you yourself wish to share is of absolute value. But we are surely correct in rejecting this shallow and self-serving message. Indeed, in his Enthronement Sermon of 1991, Archbishop George Carey himself spoke out against this view at one point when he was addressing, as it were, representatives of the non-Christian faiths:

> The faith that I have in Christ and His good news is so important that I am compelled—necessity is laid upon me—to share it with all people. But I trust I can listen to your story and respect your integrity, even though having listened I may still want to offer you, as to all, the claims of my Lord.

This is the precise challenge which must be met if Jewish evangelism is to be accorded integrity in today's world. Does the fact that you are convinced that Jewish people need the Gospel, necessarily mean that you will be insensitive to the full range of their needs? Will it mean that you believe that you have nothing to learn from Jewish people and traditions? Is it the case that you can only be opposed to antisemitism, or that you can only be fully supportive of the right of the State of Israel to exist, if you are also anti-evangelical? Is it really impossible to be committed to both dialogue and evangelism? Let us now outline the issues involved by an examination of the most significant terms and concepts found in the debate about the legitimacy of Jewish evangelism.

# MISSION

When the word mission is used in a Jewish context, the spectre of forced conversions and rice Christians appears. As mentioned in the previous chapter, the popular understanding is that neither the missionary nor the Jewish person listening to him/her has an ounce of integrity. This in turn is based on the assumption that the Gospel could not possibly attract a Jewish person for truth's sake alone. This assumption is to be rejected out of hand! There is a growing (in fact accelerating) number of Jewish people who are coming to faith in Jesus, all of whom have made decisions of faith based on the genuine conviction that he is the Messiah. It must also be stressed that for very many of them it has been a commitment which has meant considerable personal cost, the opposite of personal aggrandisement, social acceptance or freedom from intolerance.

Of course the very concept of mission is generally out of vogue in today's Western societies, and mission is easily caricatured as the activity of insensitive, aggressive people. It is sadly true that many examples could be given of individuals who seem to fit the stereotype; Christians who have no real sensitivity to Jewish people, and who seem to lack any real humility. But one cannot judge a community by the mavericks who live and operate on its margins. It was in recognition of the harm done by lone Christians operating without any accountability, that a good number of Jewish missions and organisations, dedicated not only to evangelism but also to the support of Jewish believers in Jesus, began to draw up written codes of practice so that people would be able to differentiate them from such individuals.

One such example of a code of practice comes from an organisation mentioned above: CMJ. In particular, CMJ distances itself from six practices which it, along with others, is often accused of breaching, though it must be said that no evidence is ever produced to substantiate the accusations made occasionally in the media. The practices mentioned here are rejected by all the church-based missions in fact. These are the approaches which are categorically condemned by CMJ:

1. Inviting people to events and activities under false pretences.
2. Dressing up or posing as something we are not in order to hide our true identities...
3. Using illegitimate or unfair means of persuasion such as manipulation, brainwashing...
4. Failing to make known the full implications and consequences of becoming a disciple of Jesus.
5. Involvement in discussion with minors without the knowledge of parents or guardians.
6. Offering any form of financial or material gain as an inducement.

It is often said in the Jewish media and from Jewish pulpits that evangelicals, and in particular agencies dedicated to Jewish evangelism, are characteristically engaged in these kinds of activity, but this is simply not true. The rhetoric has proved successful in many quarters, sadly, and large numbers of people have been deceived into believing that such unethical conduct is the daily round of evangelicals and Jewish believers in Jesus. On the occasions when these accusations have been challenged, and the accusers pressed to provide evidence or trustworthy witnesses to substantiate the rhetoric, nothing has been forthcoming.

What we must realise is that it is because of the awful nature of Jewish-Christian relations in the past that such accusations are still made by Jewish people. It is because of that past history that organisations like CMJ have to make such statements at all about their ethical conduct.

There is no doubt that the finest ambassadors for Jesus among Jewish people are those who take plenty of time to get to know the people, who do a lot of listening, and only then begin to share their testimony about the Jewishness of Jesus and his relevance for the Jewish people today.

It is also because of the unique relationship between Israel and the Church that Christians need to be specially prepared to be effective witnesses in a Jewish context. Jewish people cannot be treated in the same way as Muslims, Hindus, or anyone else, and so Christians see specialist preparation for sharing the Gospel with Jewish people as a positive and sensitive exercise. Others tend to label it with the pejorative expression, 'targetting the Jewish people'. This conveys the message that specialist organisations which serve to help the churches appreciate the Jewish people, and learn how to share their faith sensitively with Jewish people, are actually groups of fanatics out to seduce and deceive the Jewish community. Christians must learn to respond firmly, yet graciously, to this accusation. The Church is, by definition, a missionary society, and the determination to relate the Gospel to Jewish people in culturally sensitive ways is meant as a positive, not a negative act.

## PROSELYTISM

This term began life simply as a synonym for evangelism. However, it has come to be used in a much more particular way by people involved in the various inter-faith movements. It has in practice become synonymous with the notions of coercion and manipulation. In 1973 Billy Graham felt the need to disassociate himself from the possibility of this kind of accusation by saying that he was opposed to 'coercive proselytising' of Jewish people, these two words having become almost inseparable in many people's minds. But *all* of us should be opposed to any form of pressure being placed on people, or any type of exploitation of people's weaknesses.

Which Christian would not agree with the declaration of the World Council of Churches that Christians must condemn

> whatever violates the right of the human person ... to be free from external coercion in religious matters, or whatever, in the proclamation of the Gospel, does not conform to the ways God draws free men to himself...

And what word does the WCC use to express this attitude which we must condemn? Yes, the word is proselytism. We see exactly the same thing in the Statement of Vatican Two that

Proselytism is a corruption of Christian witness by appealing to hidden forms of coercion or by a style of propaganda unworthy of the gospel. It is not the use but the abuse of religious freedom.

But why mention this matter at all? Because there is plenty of scope for confusion when some people use the word simply to mean evangelism, whereas others use it to mean unethical forms of evangelism. Indeed what we find nowadays is that opponents of 'evangelism' amongst Jewish people regularly refer to it by the word 'proselytism', knowing full well that it will be understood by many in this negative sense of unscrupulous manipulation or coercion of the weak and vulnerable. So one might read in a newspaper that a church has been 'proselytising' Jewish people in its parish, giving the impression to many that some type of unethical behaviour has been involved, whereas all it means is that local Christians have been legally, morally and sensitively speaking to Jewish people about the Gospel. If challenged on the use of this highly emotive term, such a person can simply say that they only meant to say 'evangelism', and that they cannot be blamed if others misinterpreted them.

Other individuals and organisations hide behind this confusion in another way. They may not actually believe that evangelism among Jewish people is absolutely out of the question, but they do want to appear to be against any form of organised evangelism, and so they say publically that they are categorically opposed to proselytism. Now it can be interpreted that this means that they are against evangelism, but in fact they need only have said that they are against coercion and exploitation.

Christians must be on their guard against this hijacking of the term by people who wish to give the impression that all evangelism among Jewish people involves unethical conduct. Christians must also be outspoken in their own public (and private) condemnation of any unethical or unacceptable motives or methods in evangelism.

## WITNESS

Many Christians today prefer this term to any other, feeling that it sounds less aggressive than the terms mission, proselytism, or even evangelism. A witness is simply someone who bears witness; who gives his/her testimony of what he/she saw, experienced, etc. Giving your testimony to what you have found to be true in your own life is viewed as being non-threatening, and therefore more socially acceptable. But even here there is opposition from some quarters. Rabbi Daniel Polish reflects the position of many when he distinguishes between what he calls 'active' and 'passive' witness. What constitutes the difference between the two types of witness?

> Active witness consists of actions directed toward another...to win someone else over to my faith. Passive witness is inner-directed...done with no consideration for the effect...on some other...

This concept of passive witness, which he maintains is the only authentic one, is not in fact compatible with the New Testament's own understanding of bearing witness to the Lord. In the book of Acts, for instance, there is a clearly discernable pattern in the testimonies of Peter and Paul, involving not only certain basic truths regarding Jesus' life, death and resurrection, but also a call to repentance, a promise of forgiveness, and an appeal to believe this which is made to the Jewish people first. The witnesses in the New Testament are all trying to *persuade* their hearers of the truth about Jesus. Evangelicals today will want to maintain that their witness must also be given with the hope for positive responses to Jesus. This does not mean that any pressure will be put upon people, nor that positive responses will be looked for after every conversation, but that the over-all hope of the Christian is that at some point the other person will come to experience the same relationship with Jesus him/herself.

I am convinced that it *is* possible, with theological and personal integrity, to be involved in both witness and dialogue. Our testimony to Jesus as the Messiah has a strong rhythmic quality as it moves graciously and purposefully between the *retrospective* movement of learning about God from Israel and the *prospective* movement of witnessing about God to Israel. We just cannot treat the Jewish people as if they were pagans. They base themselves on the same promises of salvation, and stand on many of the same acts of God as Christians. Hence we need to be reminded of passages like John 4:22 (salvation is from the Jews); Romans 9:4–5 (Theirs is the adoption as sons...the promises...); 11:29 (God's gifts and his call are irre-vocable). Hence we need to be both listening and learning from Jewish traditions and Jewish people.

On the other hand, there is only one Gospel, which must not be distorted or abandoned, so that we dare not forget passages like Galatians 1:6–8 (a different gospel—which is really no gospel at all); Ephesians 4:4 (There is one body and one Spirit); Romans 1:16 (first for the Jew, then for the Gentile). The same Gospel is for Jew and non-Jew alike.

Therefore, if I may coin a phrase, Christians must be involved in this 'rhythm of witness', a recognition of continuity and discontinuity, of receiving and giving, of being changed and of seeking to change. Many voices will tell us that this is impossible, and that it is even unethical to attempt it, but this is not true. It is not illegitimate for the Church to bind together in one Bible both the Hebrew Testament and the New Testament, recognising the tension and interplay of continuity and discontinuity. Of course some Jewish (and even Christian) voices have tried to speak against the Church's adoption of the Hebrew Scriptures as part of the Christian Bible, but the Church has maintained its canon.

Both CCJ and CMJ, to continue to use these organisations as good examples, would insist that it is impossible to understand the New Testament fully without the Hebrew Scriptures. Let it not be said that evangelicals do not affirm this basic truth. However, CMJ would go further and insist that it is equally impossible to understand the Hebrew Scriptures fully without the New Testament. When a Christian is reading the New Testament, this 'rhythm of witness' comes into play. The Christian needs the insights which can only come from a correct reading, and interpretation, of the Hebrew

Scriptures, but at the same time, he/she must pay full attention to the New Testament's insights with regard to the overall biblical revelation. In the same way, it is surely a mark of Christian maturity to be looking for insights to receive from, as well as to share with, Jewish tradition and Jewish people.

## CONVERSION

Here is yet another term which causes the hackles to rise when it is used in a Jewish context. Biblically speaking, conversion is a response to God's grace and will, resulting in faith, repentance, obedience and new life. It is a complete turning around of one's life, in which the focus is away from oneself towards God. What could the objection be to this concept?

The point can be made dramatically by quoting one of the founders of the modern Jewish-Christian Dialogue movement, James Parkes, an Anglican clergyman of a generation ago:

> We have failed to convert the Jews, and we shall always fail, because it is not the will of God that they shall *become Gentile Christians*. (emphasis mine)

Here is the issue in a nutshell. Because of the terrible history of Jewish-Christian relations over the centuries, and because the Church has traditionally insisted that Jews who become Christians (whether from conviction or expediency) must renounce their Jewishness, all of which we have already looked at, then the common understanding has arisen that when a Jewish person 'becomes a Christian' he/she also thereby leaves the Jewish community and becomes a Gentile. 'Conversion' is taken to refer to this process whereby such a Jewish person abandons, and is lost to, the Jewish community. The meaning of conversion as inner transformation has been left far behind.

How should we respond to this? There are two things which must be said: a) We agree that it is definitely *not* the will of God that Jewish people should cease to be Jewish, adopting instead all of the thought patterns, customs and traditions of various Gentile cultures. b) It is nonetheless true that in spite of this first point, it *is* the will of God that Jewish people should recognise Jesus to be Israel's one and only Messiah.

This brings us to one of the most fundamental issues in the whole area of Jewish-Christian relations. In the next chapter we shall be looking at the subject of the identity and lifestyle of Jewish people who become disciples of Jesus. As we shall see, their own testimony is that they remain Jewish when they accept Jesus as their Messiah. This is also the conviction of Gentile Christians who are actively involved in witnessing to Jewish people. Jewish people are assured that they will remain Jewish even if they come to accept Jesus as their Messiah. This is not an evangelical gimmick, nor a deceptive strategy, as opponents charge, but a genuinely held theological and missiological conviction.

Perhaps a couple of quotes from Jewish Believers will help to spell this out for us:

One should always remember that the faith he is

> sharing originated with Jews. A Jewish person who accepts Jesus as his Messiah does not 'convert to another religion', but actually returns to the faith of Abraham, Isaac and Jacob *fulfilled*. (Chosen People Ministries)

> Don't call me a converted Jew. I never converted from being Jewish, but I was converted from sin— and being Jewish was never a sin! (Moishe Rosen)

We must be very sensitive, therefore, to the implications of the term 'conversion'. We must be careful to make it clear that we challenge and reject the interpretation given to it that it means to cease to be Jewish and a member of the Jewish people. On the other hand, the biblical reality which lies behind the proper use of the term must not be lost in the debate. A Jewish person who has his/her faith *fulfilled* in relationship with Jesus will also have his/her heart *converted* in the personal and radical re-orientation of life from self to God.

It will have become obvious to the reader that all of the above issues and perspectives are uniquely significant to the question of the relationship between the Church and the Jewish people. It is because of the unique nature of Christianity's relationship to Judaism, that there are such problems within the churches as how to see the proper attitude which Christians should have towards Jewish people. In what sense can we have a mission to Israel, in which we also remember that we are taking back to her the very treasure which we received from her? This is not a problem vis-a-vis any other faith community. In the same way, there is no other faith community for which it could be said that they are directly fulfilling their explicit scriptural beliefs by believing in Jesus.

What we must now do in this overview of the special relationship between Israel and the Church is to look at the rapidly growing community of Messianic Jews, those Jewish people who have accepted Jesus as their Messiah, Saviour and Lord. What could be more natural than that a Jewish person follow Jesus?

# 7
# Are Messianic Jews The Key?

It is surprising how little attention is given in the books and articles dealing with Jewish-Christian relations, to the subject of Jewish people who become followers of Jesus. A large percentage of the works do not mention them at all, whereas many others simply note that there are such people, implying that they are a marginalised group of inadequate people with no significance whatsoever. Looked at another way, I suppose it is not so surprising, since they pose a threat to all of those Jewish and Christian people who wish to keep the Gospel separate from the Jewish community. Nonetheless it may still take evangelicals by surprise to learn that many Christian leaders and theologians are quite antipathetic to Jewish believers.

From the Christian perspective, the triumphalistic teaching that the Church has superseded Israel in all things has bred a total refusal to see anything positive in the Jewishness of Jewish people who become

followers of Jesus, and join local congregations of
worshippers. From the Jewish perspective, the teaching that such people have betrayed the memory of
Jewish martyrs and joined the camp of the enemy,
has led to the situation where all Jewish believers are
pre-judged to have sold out to Christian bribes or
fallen victim to Christian entrapment. We have
looked at these issues in previous chapters.

Jewish followers of Jesus are therefore an anomaly
to both of the faith communities. It is an inescapable
fact of history, however, that there has always been a
steady stream of genuine Jewish believers from the
days of Jesus, the Jew, right up to today. Sometimes
this stream has actually become strong and fast-
moving, and at present we are living in a time of
great growth and self-confidence among them. From
the 1960s, a new determination has come into the
movement, and Jewish believers are asserting their
right to be who they are; their right to speak about
who they are; and their right to be accepted as they
are by others.

Spokesmen for the movement often describe it
with a metaphor from the world of photography. Just
as one must reserve judgement on a photograph until
it is finally developed, in the same way one must not
make hard and fast judgements on Messianic Jews
while the movement is still in its infancy. What, then,
is God doing in this community? Can we actually
speak of a 'movement' of Jewish believers when so
many Christians and Jewish people have never come
across them?

It may be helpful to begin by looking at the very
terms used by Jewish believers to describe them-

selves. The term which I have used consistently throughout this book is 'Jewish believer', a term broadly acceptable as a sort of neutral description. But, historically speaking, there are really two different groups of Jewish believers, a reality reflected in the terms usually used by each group. These chosen terms are, on the one hand, 'Hebrew Christian' or 'Jewish Christian', and on the other hand, 'Messianic Jew'. What are the reasons for the personal or cultural preferences in these self-designations? The whole thing may seem like little more than playing with words to some Christians, but as Menachem Benhayim, the Israel Secretary of the International Messianic Jewish (Hebrew Christian) Alliance, writes:

> What may only seem like semantic preferences, eg usages of terms like Messianic in place of Christian, represent serious psychological, social and intellectual concerns.

Some Jewish believers maintain that they are equally happy with either term, but for the majority it is very important that their particular self-understanding be known and respected. How are the terms used? In any phrase used by Jewish believers there will be a noun and an adjective. The noun is the basic information-carrying word, while the adjective, though important, serves to further clarify or describe the noun. For example, we could compare the two descriptions of someone as either a Palestinian freedom-fighter (thus his supporters) or as a Palestinian terrorist (thus his enemies). The difference is immediately clear. In this light we can point out the following emphases which are there in the two terms for Jewish believers:

> A Messianic Jew, who insists on this term, believes it to be of fundamental importance to let it be known that he/she is a Jewish person; and further, that he/she is a special type of Jew, one who is a disciple of Jesus, rather than belonging to Orthodox or Reform ideologies, etc.

> A Hebrew Christian, who insists on this term, believes it to be of fundamental importance to let it be known that he/she is a Christian, happily identified with the term and with the worldwide (Gentile dominated) Church; and further, that he/she is Jewish by ethnic origin, not Gentile.

There are three broad factors involved in the different emphases of the two wings of the movement of Jewish believers:

a) A search for an indigenous expression of theology, worship and lifestyle for Jewish believers within the whole Church.

b) A search for an appropriate evangelistic strategy which will reach Jewish people with the Good News that Jesus is their Messiah.

c) A vision to help the whole Church rediscover its own Jewish roots.

Hebrew Christians, who have traditionally joined local church congregations (whether by choice or direction) often have an interest in the third area, though this is by no means true of them all. It is not common to find them actively involved in any sort of planning or working for the first two areas. What often happens is that Hebrew Christians meet regularly for prayer and fellowship, focussing largely on their own concerns and needs, but by no means adopting a high profile.

Messianic Jewish groups and congregations, on the other hand, are firmly committed to the first two areas of concern, and many of them would also give some priority to helping the churches around them return to their Jewish roots. Their distinctiveness, though, lies in the twin vision of being an authentic Jewish expression of New Testament faith, worship and lifestyle, and also of being an effective evangelistic base for witnessing to Jewish people.

There are two aspects to the first concern of the Messianic Jewish communities. First of all there is the commitment to preventing cultural and personal assimilation to Gentilised forms of worship and behaviour. Most Christians do not appreciate the pressures on Jewish believers in our churches to fit in with all of the ways of the non-Jewish majority. It is understandable, I suppose, that individuals are encouraged to learn to fit in with the majority view, and so our churches contribute, however unknowingly, to the gradual assimilation of Hebrew Christians. There are many thousands of Jewish believers in our churches whose identity is hardly known, if at all, even within their congregations. For that matter there are not a few Hebrew Christian clergy in the various denominations too, people usually without any interest in their own Jewishness.

Secondly there is the concern to give full support to Messianic Jews, encouraging them in their new faith, and helping them to mature in their new life.

Churches don't deliberately neglect Jewish believers, it is just that they do not know how to counsel them with their particular problems and hopes. John Bell, a Messianic Jewish pastor in the USA, also draws attention to another type of problem altogether which faces Jewish believers in some churches:

> those who are super-semitic expect Messianic Jews to be Bible scholars and 100% sanctified, almost from the day of their salvation. Their affection for the Jewish people is romantic and well-intentioned, but it causes problems for the young Jewish believer who is elevated in an unnatural fashion.

There had been a few sporadic attempts before the present century to establish Messianic Jewish congregations of one sort or another. Only since the end of the Second World War, however, have the political and social climates in the West been such as to provide the freedom for Jewish believers to really speak out clearly and without fear of reprisals on their own behalf. This reflects in large part the newly-found social and political freedoms of Western Jewry as a whole. It is now possible for numbers of Jewish believers, along with non-Jewish Christian friends and supporters, to form their own congregations, and to begin to develop their own particular identities, liturgies, worship songs and dances.

Another significant factor has been the growing acceptance by missionary and church leaders of what is known as the principle of 'contextualisation'. There is widespread sympathy for the desire of Christians everywhere to develop expressions of Christian worship and lifestyle which best reflect the contexts, traditions and needs of their own particular culture or sub-culture. We see the encouragement given to so-called 'Chinese churches' or 'Arabic churches', for example. The climate is right for the development of Messianic Jewish congregations. Indeed it is this Messianic Jewish wing of the whole movement of Jewish believers which is at the heart of the movement's current expansion.

At this point, however, it is vital to point out that there is no sense of division or enmity between the two wings of the movement. There are definite differences between them, but they are united in their common love for the Messiah, and in their shared struggles as Jewish believers trying to relate lovingly to the Jewish community as well as to the churches.

Our Messianic Jewish brothers and sisters are in real need of our support and prayers. From the churches we continue to hear accusations that Messianic Judaism (with its Messianic Jewish congregations) is just another modern deviant cult, a cult which will involve the typical symptoms of authoritarian leadership, opposition to the Church, ethnic exclusivity, religious legalism and brainwashing. These charges are simply not true. There are differences of emphasis and style among the various congregations, as one would expect, since that is the same situation with our churches. Messianic Judaism is certainly not a cult movement. Congregations are open to full membership by both Jews and non-Jews, and leadership positions, including those of pastor and elder, are regularly held by non-Jewish believers.

What about the issue of keeping the Law (the

Torah)? When Messianic Jews are living in accordance with Jewish traditions and the like, are they not committing the sin of 'Judaising'? It is perfectly plain throughout the Bible that salvation is a free gift from God, and that is never depended upon the keeping of the laws of God. However, once people are in a covenant relationship with God (and this applies equally to Israel and the Church), then adherence to and obedience to the laws of God are demanded as full obligations. But such obedience is not the *basis* of God's love or choice. Furthermore, the New Testament makes it clear that there is no need for believers to adhere to the Jewish traditions regarding the full and proper keeping of the Torah. Not even Jewish believers need to practise the rabbinic laws of keeping kosher, etc. It is stressed that any teaching which suggests that all of this is necessary is false teaching. This is not in dispute, and Messianic Jews make it clear that they do not see their lifestyle as in any way related to their salvation.

The issue is that Messianic Jews claim the freedom to live their lives as *Jewish* people who believe in Jesus. They want to live their lives within the Jewish community, enjoying their Jewish ways and customs, their Jewish food and music, as far as is possible, without in any way compromising the truths of the Gospel. Keeping the Sabbath as a day without work, declining to eat pork, and so on, are surely all right if not done out of some sense of their necessity for salvation or some attitude of one-upmanship. The God of Abraham, Isaac and Jacob, the Father of our Lord Jesus, is assuredly not anti-Jewish!

From the Jewish community we also hear strong

accusations about the lack of integrity of Messianic Jewish people. In fact the Jewish reactions of today tend to be the same as those which were decreed to be normative by Judaism's founding leaders. Even though the political and social contexts of Western Jewry have changed very much for the better, today's leaders still propagate the line that Jewish believers in Jesus cannot be acting out of religious conviction and conscience. They must be motivated by either fear for their safety or a desire for public advancement. Messianic Jews are therefore branded, without fair trial, as traitors to the vulnerable Jewish community. What is more, they are considered to be unscrupulous deceivers, who exploit and manipulate common Jewish symbols and language in order to fool Jews and Christians alike into the belief that one can be Jewish and a believer in Jesus at the same time. Let it be clearly said that none of these accusations is true!

Our Messianic Jewish brothers and sisters in Jesus are very much in need of our prayers and support. Many Church leaders are dismissing them as heretics or as a cult group, insisting that they prove their true Christian pedigree, if indeed they have one, by giving up their Jewishness and joining a church, learning to live like a non-Jew. Most Jewish community leaders are condemning them as immoral self-seekers, or marginalising them as pathetic inadequates. Things have not changed much over the generations. Since the 4th century, both the Church and the Synagogue, for their own reasons, have consistently insisted that Jewish believers abandon their claim to Jewishness. The

Church's anti-Judaism and anti-Semitism have dictated its agenda, while the Jewish community maintains that Messianic Jews have committed the sin of self-alienation.

We need to stand with the Messianic Jewish community in its own response that there is a need to differentiate between the two issues of Jewishness and Judaism. It is undoubtedly true that they have rejected other forms of Judaism in favour of the one form of Judaism which is centred on Jesus as Israel's Messiah. But this does not mean that they have stopped being Jewish people. It is also undeniably true that they refuse to do what most of their predecessors were forced to do, namely to accept a Gentile expression of the biblical faith and life as being the only one acceptable to God. This does not mean that they are somehow sub-Christian. When Jesus returns, Jewish people will realise that Messianic Jews were right about him, and Christians will discover that they had re-made him altogether too much in their own Gentile images!

Where are these Messianic Jewish communities? No-one knows exactly how many Jewish believers there are altogether, since very many of them have chosen to keep their Jewishness to themselves, becoming regular members of local Christian congregations, and living just like everyone else. This has as much to do with their experience and memory of prejudice against Jewish people by Christians, as it has to do with any positive theological choice. Another reason that no-one knows the total number of Jewish believers is that there are also many Jewish people who have become believers but who are too afraid of family or community reactions to declare their faith publicly. This phenomenon of secret believers is not unique to the Jewish scene of course, but it is important that Christians are aware of the part it plays in this context too.

Having said all this, there are approximately 100,000 known Jewish believers in the USA; several thousand in Canada; thousands in South America; perhaps 800 to 1,000 in Britain; some hundreds in France, as in the CIS, other countries in Eastern Europe, South Africa and Australia; and last but not least, about 4,000 in Israel. Let me stress that these are simply figures for the number of publicly known Jewish believers. There are well over 120 Messianic Jewish congregations in North America, and 36 in Israel, with other countries having a few each. On top of this, there is also a growing number of house fellowships which have not taken the step yet of forming themselves into full congregations.

Until both the Christian and the Jewish communities are able to meet with the Messianic Jewish community on the basis of respect for its integrity and identity, then we may never see a proper relationship of mutual respect and co-operation between Jews and Christians at all. At least not between Jewish people and those Christians who belong to the evangelical base of the Church. To this extent it may not be too much to claim that Messianic Jews are the key to the future.

Not only that, of course, but if the claims of Messianic Jews and their non-Jewish Christian supporters are correct, then we may be witnessing one of the signs of God's increased intervention in history, in accordance with the words of the apostle Paul, that some day 'all Israel will be saved' (Rom 11:26). Is God calling us back to Jesus' parable of the wise and foolish virgins, encouraging us to be ready, to be discerning the signs of the age?

# CONCLUSION

It really has been the intention of this short study to motivate Christians to serious thinking about the relationship between Israel and the Church. Hopefully, the point has been taken that our relationship with Jewish people is quite unique. We are family, and family quarrels are always much more complex and hurtful than any others. There are different Christian attitudes to this relationship, ranging from rejecting all things Jewish as intolerable, to that which is convinced that Christians have far more of value to learn from Jewish religious traditions than they have to offer. Evangelicals must learn to appreciate the insights of the various forms of Judaism, and must certainly come to the point of genuine repentance for Christian antisemitism. At the same time we must never lose sight of the fact that Jesus is Israel's one and only Messiah, and that our biblical mandate is to share this truth with the Jewish people in every generation.

Without doubt there is much for each to learn from the other, in theological matters as well as in issues of social justice. Nor can it be doubted that both have played their part in the mutual estrangement that now exists between the two communities, though the overwhelming responsibility for this lies with the churches. Yet again we must mention the harm done by both the Synagogue and the Church to the community of Jewish believers in Jesus. It is time for a real meeting of minds and spirits, for an authentic dialogue among mature faith communities, and we can all thank God that this is happening to a fair degree already. But dialogue must not be allowed to proceed *at the expense of* the Church's distinctive witness to the uniqueness of Jesus.

What is so special about the Jewish people? They are the people whom God chose to be His servants, witnessing to the truth of His claims for Himself, and also to the fact of His claims on all of humanity. God's covenant commitment to the Jewish people, given through Abraham, is still valid, and Jewish people who confess that Jesus is Messiah and Lord are the double heirs of Abraham. As Paul says to the Church:

> if their transgression means riches for the world, and their loss means riches for the Gentiles, how much greater riches will their fulness bring!...I do not want you to be ignorant of this mystery, brothers, so that you may not be conceited: Israel has experienced a hardening in part until the full number of the Gentiles has come in. And so all Israel will be saved...for God's gifts and his call are irrevocable (Rom 11:12, 25–26a, 29).

God called Israel, in Abraham, to be the channel of His blessing to all the nations of the earth (Gen 12:3; Is 42:6). When the time came for the long-promised Messiah of Israel to come to earth, God permitted a hardness of heart to come over Israel so that the Good News that he is also the saviour of the whole world would explode into the whole world. God's intention now is that the Church, called out from all of the peoples of the world (and that includes Israel, of course), will make Israel as a whole jealous (Rom 11:11, 14) for what is also hers—namely a full relationship with the God who called her into being all those generations ago:

> How, then, can they call on the one they have not believed in? And how can they believe in the one of whom they have not heard? And how can they hear without someone preaching to them? (Rom 10:14).

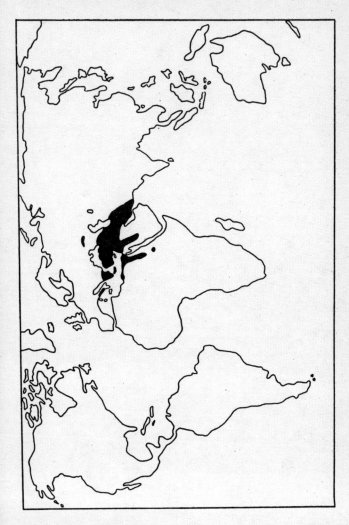

**THE TIME OF JESUS**

300 AD

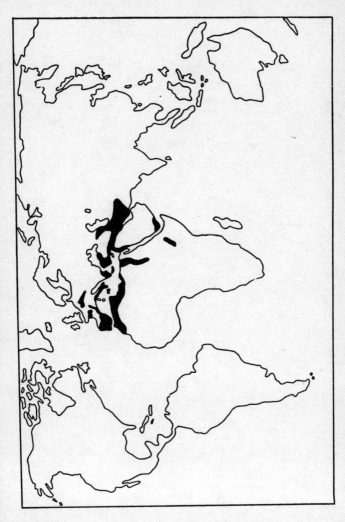

**900 AD**

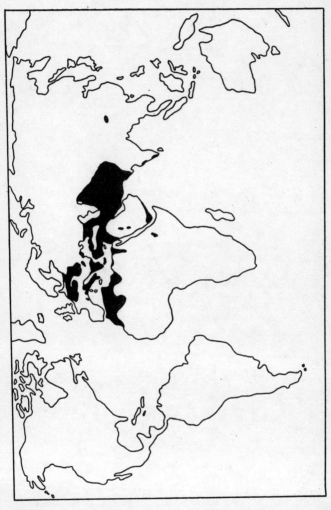

**1500 AD**

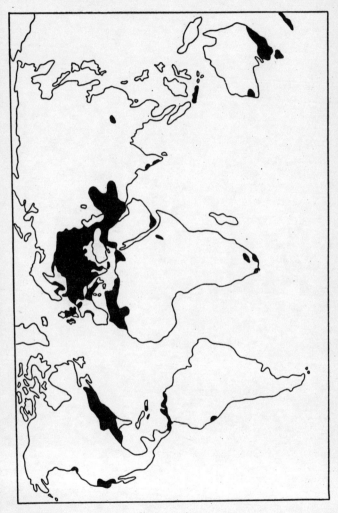

**1880 AD**

**THE PRESENT DAY**

# BIBLIOGRAPHY

The following list of books is intended to provide suitable material for further study by those who have been stimulated to more work in the area of Jewish-Christian relations by reading the present book. For maximum help it was decided to give separate material for each chapter.

## INTRODUCTION

Harrelson, Walter and Randall M. Falk: *Jews and Christians. A Troubled Family* (Abingdon Press, 1990)

Jocz, Jacob: *The Jewish People and Jesus Christ* (Baker, 1949)

Klenicki, Leon and Richard John Neuhaus: *Believing Today. Jew and Christian in Conversation* (Eerdmans, 1989)

Tanenbaum, Marc H., Marvin R. Wilson, and A. James Rudin: *Evangelicals and Jews in Conversation* (Baker, 1978)

158 / *The Covenant With The Jews*

HOW LONG DOES GOD'S CHOICE LAST?

Boadt, Laurence, Helga Croner and Leon Klenicki (eds.): *Biblical Studies: Meeting Ground of Jews and Christians* (Paulist Press, 1980)

Croner, Helga and Leon Klenicki: *Issues in the Jewish-Christian Dialogue: Jewish Perspectives on Covenant, Mission and Witness* (Paulist Press, 1978)

Wilson, Marvin R.: *Our Father Abraham. Jewish Roots of the Christian Faith* (Eerdmans, 1989)


BIBLICAL PROPHECIES AND MODERN POLITICS

Torrance, David W.: *The Witness of the Jews to God* (The Handsel Press, 1982)

Riggans, Walter: *Israel and Zionism* (The Handsel Press, 1988)


ARE ANY OF YOUR BEST FRIENDS JEWISH?

Cohn-Sherbok, Dan: *The Crucified Jew. Twenty Centuries of Christian Anti-Semitism* (Harper Collins, 1992)

Parkes, James: *The Conflict of the Church and the Synagogue* (Hermon Press, 1974)

Rausch, David A.: *A Legacy of Hatred. Why Christians Must Not Forget the Holocaust* (2nd. edition, Baker, 1990)

Stevens, George: *Strife Between Brothers* (Olive Press, 1979)


'FIRST FOR THE JEW, THEN FOR THE GENTILE'!

Jocz, Jacob: *The Jewish People and Jesus Christ After Auschwitz* (Baker, 1981)

Rosen, Moishe: *Y'shua: The Jewish Way to Say Jesus* (Moody Press, 1982)

ARE MESSIANIC JEWS THE KEY?

Fischer, John: *The Olive Tree Connection* (rev. ed., IVP, 1983)

Juster, Daniel: *Jewish Roots: A Foundation of Biblical Theology for Messianic Judaism* (Davar Publishing, 1986)

Stern, David H.: *Messianic Jewish Manifesto* (Jewish New Testament Publications, 1988)